MYTHOLOGY

Roni Jay

TEACH YOURSELF BOOKS

Dedication

For Ra

Long-renowned as the authoritative source for self-guided learning – with more than 30 million copies sold worldwide – the *Teach Yourself* series includes over 200 titles in the fields of languages, crafts, hobbies, sports, and other leisure activities.

A catalogue record for this title is available from the British Library.

Library of Congress Catalog Card Number: on file.

First published in UK 1996 by Hodder Headline Plc, 338 Euston Road, London NW1 3BH

First published in US 1996 by NTC Publishing Group, 4255 West Touchy Avenue, Lincolnwood (Chicago), Illinois 60646 – 1975 U.S.A.

Copyright © 1996 Roni Jay

Typeset by Transet Limited, Coventry, England.
Printed in England by Cox & Wyman Limited, Reading, Berkshire.

Impression number   10 9   8   7   6   5   4   3   2   1
Year   2000   1999   1998 1997   1996

CONTENTS

1

HOW MYTHOLOGY WORKS

Five thousand years ago, the people of Mesopotamia in the Middle East invented a completely new technique: writing. To start with, they used it to record stocks and transactions; then they found new uses for it. Five hundred years later they began to write down stories about the gods and goddesses they believed in. These were the first written myths; but they were far from being the first myths ever.

Virtually every culture in the world, past or present, has a mythology of some kind. In other words, it has stories about the things it believes in, that contain a supernatural element. These stories are generally attempts to explain a fact of some kind. For example a myth may give a reason for the fact that the sun rises and sets each day; or the fact that the world exists; or an explanation of how the people who follow the myth came to be living where they do. These myths are almost always part of a broader religion: the worship of some kind of spiritual power, involving ritual observances and ceremonies. So you could say that mythology is a subset of religion; it's the collection of stories at the centre of the religion.

So why is mythology such an enduringly interesting subject? Well, for a start almost every mythology is packed with rollicking good stories. But mythology is far more than that. It is a fascinating insight into the people who develop these belief systems. It tells us a huge amount about how these people lived and where they came from. To give an example, let's go back to the early Mesopotamians. They had gods whose worship covered a wide area, and local gods of individual cities. The people of Babylonia, who had successfully risen to power in the region, had a creation myth (see Chapter 2, page 21), in which their local god defeated the supreme mother goddess to become overall ruler of the gods, raised from local to national status. This is an allegory that is actually telling us that Babylon defeated the controlling power of the region, and the Babylonians were elevated to become the dominant power in that part of the world.

Here's another very different example of how mythology can tell you about the culture it derives from. The Chinese pantheon (a collective noun meaning all the gods of a mythology) is arranged in an incredibly complex bureaucratic hierarchy, where every deity has a clearly defined job description and a system for making regular reports to the senior deity of that 'department'. This is a clear reflection of Chinese society. You might argue that the mythology is only telling us what we know already. But when you study the mythology of cultures that no longer exist, as with the Babylonians, these clues to their social structures can be incredibly useful.

So how do we know about ancient mythologies? There are several possible sources, some more reliable than others. Most helpful of all is when cultures leave written records behind them, as the Mesopotamians did. To add to this evidence, they may also leave us other clues, such as artefacts which depict gods and goddesses, or rituals, or even tell stories: paintings on vases, sculptures, carvings and so on.

Then there are the clues that other people pass on. The Greek and Roman writers, for example, told us a great deal about the Celts. This information is certainly helpful, but it has to be treated with a degree of caution. The problem is that many of these writers were biased. The Romans thought that the Celts were savages, and although they recorded the Celts' religious ceremonies with fascination, the Romans seem to have considered their beliefs largely unworthy of study. So they tell us a great deal about what the Celts did, but relatively little about *why* they did it. To give another example, the Viking myths were all recorded by Christian monks, so you have to be on the lookout for any Christian ideas that the monks may have been tempted to add as they transcribed the myths.

———— **The function of myths** ————

People don't invent myths for the fun of it. They may enjoy the stories – in fact, the more they enjoy the stories the more they will identify with them – but mythologies have a deeper significance than mere entertainment. They perform a function. Some myths perform several functions at once. There are eight key reasons why any particular mythology may have developed:

1 To explain natural phenomena. Many myths exist to answer the questions that everyone asks sooner or later, such as why the crops die every winter, or where the sun goes at night.

2 To control natural forces. Once you have gods, you can influence them by making sacrifices, offering prayers or performing rituals. This means that you have a slightly better chance of arranging for the rain to fall when you need it, or of curing diseases.

3 To bind a clan, tribe or nation together. A shared mythology is a strong social tie. In fact, it was about the only thing that really unified the Greek empire.

4 To record historical events. Many events in a tribe's or nation's history are recorded in a mythologised form. For example, the two great rivers of Mesopotamia, the Tigris and the Euphrates, were prone to flood dangerously and unpredictably. The Hebrew people originated in that region, and the Judaeo-Christian myth of Noah – and the almost identical Babylonian flood myth – are believed to be accounts of a particularly calamitous flood that archaeologists have identified as devastating the region in around 4000 BC.

5 To give a kind of verbal geography lesson. Before maps were drawn, myths often gave the only description of landmarks to look out for on a journey. They told you, for example, that if you crossed this mountain range you would find a narrow pass followed by a dangerous precipice, and so on – the danger was usually exaggerated, of course, for effect. The Greek myths, for example, tell that if you sail from the Mediterranean through to the Black Sea, you have to contend with the Symplegades, a pair of huge rocks that crash together, crushing ships between them. Once Jason and the Argonauts had managed to pass them in the *Argo* – the first ship ever to do so – the Symplegades became fixed. This is an exaggerated description of the steep-sided and narrow Bosporus, the straits that run past Istanbul and which connect the Mediterranean with the Black Sea. Their narrowest point is only about 500 metres across, and the currents are incredibly strong.

6 To set examples for people's behaviour. There are two types of myth that do this. Many mythologies have gods who behave in a way that their people are supposed to emulate. There are also

numerous hero-myths, which occur in most mythologies, in which a human behaves particularly courageously or nobly. Sometimes these myths are based on real historical characters, but not always. They may or may not be deified (made into gods) at the end of their heroic exploits.

7 To justify a social structure. The structure of the mythological heaven tends to reflect the social structure of the culture it belongs to. But it can be used the other way round by the king, tribal chieftain or priests, to claim that society must be ordered this way to reflect the gods' order of things. Religion and politics is always a potent combination; the Romans – to give one example of many – proclaimed their emperors as gods, which meant that their word was law.

8 To control people. This is an extension of the previous point. Once you have myths, you have something to frighten people with. You can control people not only by claiming that your authority comes from god – like the divine right of kings – but also with fear. You can threaten them with punishments in the afterlife if they don't keep in line.

The narrative element in myths is important: they need to be good stories to make sure that everyone listens to them. Originally, each clan or village had its own storyteller who learned the myths and entertained and educated the clan with them. There were also professional storytellers who travelled round the wider community and told stories in exchange for food and lodgings.

How myths grow

Mythologies grow and develop along with the cultures that generate them. Although not every developed culture has necessarily gone through every single phase, there is a clear pattern. This means that the type of mythology a culture leaves behind can often tell you how far the culture developed.

Stages of development

Animism

The first stage of mythic development involves a simple belief that everything has a spirit or soul – a kind of personality – from animals and plants to rocks and fire. The sun, moon and stars, and the whole universe, are each believed to have their own spirit. You rarely, if ever, find a mythology which is at this stage because they tend to move on to the next stage fast once they begin to develop. But there are plenty of echoes of animistic beliefs in myths in which gods turn themselves into animals or plants, or are worshipped in that form (such as the Egyptian gods, who usually retained the head of the animal they had developed from).

Fetishism

This is a developed form of animism, in which an object (or fetish) is considered to be inhabited by a spirit who may be good or evil, or neutral. There is a subtle difference between this and animism in that the spirit is not an aspect of the object, but is a separate entity, and can often leave the object if it wants to (or is permitted to by the person using it). The fetish is generally of a size that means it can be carried – a bunch of feathers, perhaps, or a bone – and it becomes a kind of charm. It has the important benefit that it can be controlled, and can be instructed by the tribespeople to bring luck. If the tribes-people need a particular type of luck, the fetish may symbolise this; for example, a fetish made from dried ears of corn could be invoked to bring a good harvest. In shamanistic cultures the shaman, or medi-cine man, is the only member of the tribe who can control these spirits. A fetish is not the same thing as a god, chiefly because it is the slave and not the master of its tribe. However, a fetish may eventually, at a later stage of development, become deified if it performs its luck-bringing duties well enough.

Totemism

This is a further extension of animism, which develops to the point where each family group or clan 'adopts' a particular fetish with which it becomes identified. Frequently the clan claims some kind of descent from this totem. The classic example of totemism is in native American mythology, where each tribe would carve a totem-pole deco-rated with representations of the tribal totem. At this stage, as in all forms of animistic mythology, there is no ethical or moral dimension to the beliefs, no gods to judge, punish or reward different types of behaviour.

Polytheism

This means a belief in more than one god. Generally, the totem or fetishes perform sufficiently well that they become objects of awe and worship, rather than mere servants, and therefore become gods. There are many ways in which animistic forms of mythology become polytheistic, and in many mythologies the precise way in which it happened isn't known. However, to give you some examples of how it can happen:

- A tribe that has several fetishes may 'promote' most or all of them to become gods.
- Some gods acquire families in order to reflect the culture they come from (the ancient Egyptians couldn't imagine a god without a wife and a son).
- Some gods have different forms which come to be worshipped as different personalities. For example, many mythologies develop several sun gods, each of whom represents the sun at different stages – the rising sun, the noonday sun and so on.
- Tribes and cities combine to form larger groups – peaceably or through war – and their gods merge to form a larger pantheon. The gods of the winning side tend to be further up the hierarchy than the losers' gods.

Within polytheism there are different stages of development. Each god or goddess tends to have a particular area of responsibility – god of the sea, fertility goddess and so on. The more simple these roles are, and the more basic the function they perform (such as rain or sun), the more primitive they tend to be. Once the mythology becomes more developed it starts to introduce gods of, say, wisdom or the arts. Later still, you may find gods of specific professions or, as in Chinese mythology, a god of exams.

The more sophisticated mythologies still tend to preserve at least some of the earliest gods and goddesses; you can usually identify them by their functions. In some cases they will be gods of an earlier people, absorbed by the culture which conquered them. The Greeks, for example, were not the original settlers of their land – they conquered an earlier people and absorbed many of their gods, such as Hecate, who was a moon goddess.

Another development of polytheism which often – though not always – occurs, is that the religion of which the mythology forms a part takes on a moral or ethical dimension. The gods require their people to behave well. Before you reach this stage, the gods require their people to pay them sufficient worship but are not concerned how they act beyond that. The people perform these rites for fear of bringing down the wrath of the gods on themselves if they don't. Once the moral element enters the equation the gods are concerned with their people's behaviour towards each other as well as towards the gods themselves. Once this happens, you start to find gods who are entirely good or evil; the good ones are setting a moral example for human behaviour. And you begin to get myths in which the soul is judged after death before being sent to a place of punishment or reward.

There is one other significant way in which polytheistic religions can develop: they anthropomorphise their deities into human form. In the less-developed form – such as Egyptian mythology – gods are still worshipped in the form of their original totem, or as humans with the head of the totem (for instance, the Hindu god Ganesha has the head of an elephant). It is a natural human desire to want to create gods in our own image; it makes them less distant and far easier to relate to. The Greek writer Xenophanes of Colophon, writing around the end of the sixth century BC, said 'If cows could draw, they would make their gods in the likeness of cattle'. Sometimes the totem from which the deity developed is still discernible: the Greek goddess Athena is usually depicted accompanied by an owl – this was probably her original totem.

These developments in polytheistic religions don't necessarily all have to happen. The Greek mythology was probably the most sophisticated one never to develop the moral dimension, even though it probably absorbed the mythology of earlier people who *did* have a moralistic belief system. (Early Greek myths have some form of judgement after death, but this had disappeared by a later stage in their culture.) The Egyptians, on the other hand, had a strong ethical vein running through their mythology, but they never fully anthropomorphised their gods and goddesses – even towards the end of their civilisation.

Monotheism

A belief system that has only one god is monotheistic – Judaism, Christianity and Islam are the most obvious examples of this. Monotheism usually develops when one tribe conquers other neighbouring tribes and its god becomes top god to the point where the others are eliminated; or the chief god in the pantheon gradually absorbs all the others. These monotheistic gods generally have the power to forgive sins, and their religions tend to have the most stringent moral codes.

Why myths change

It's worth looking at the question of why myths adapt. When you first start to learn about mythology, there tends to be an impression that each mythology is frozen – a fixed set of stories. But, in fact, they can vary hugely. It's hardly surprising really, when you consider how long they are around for. Chinese mythology, for example, has existed in broadly its present form since before the time of the Roman empire.

Not only do mythologies change as time progresses, but they are simultaneously adapting from place to place. The Celts of Ireland, for example, had a different set of myths from the Celts of Britain, although they clearly belonged to the same family. These variations can be significant, but they tend to stay within certain boundaries so that they are clearly all part of the same mythology. To give you an analogy, it's rather like children's games. If you studied the rules of hopscotch among a particular group of children at a particular time, and then the rules among children 100 years previously and in a town 500 miles away, you would find significant differences. But you would know that both games were clearly variations of hopscotch.

Apart from these regional variations, there is usually a reason why a mythology makes a significant change – a reason that is often indicated in the myth itself, like the Babylonian god who caused the creation myth to change, making him supreme god, when the Babylonians gained control of the region.

As the early Indian god Indra gradually lost power to the Hindu god Vishnu, the myth in which he killed a dragon changed. In the later version, the dragon defeated Indra and he was saved only by Vishnu's intervention.

Another interesting example is the Trobriand Islanders of Melanesia. They have a creation myth in which four animals emerge from a hole in the ground in a certain order at the beginning of the world. These four animals are the totems of the four Trobriand Island clans. The order in which they emerge from the hole (according to all four of the clans) corresponds exactly with the relative status of the four clans. The animal that is the totem of the most important clan emerges first, and so on. In this type of myth, you would probably find that if the pecking-order of the clans changed, so would the order in which the animals came out of the hole.

Sometimes myths change because people's understanding increases. Suppose you believe that it rains because the rain god is happy, and you have a myth to explain why he is happy. As time goes on, you observe that it actually rains whenever the sky is full of black clouds. So you adapt your myth to incorporate an explanation of why the rain god has filled the sky with black clouds.

Once civilisations develop writing, the rate of change tends to slow down. It's true that cultures with oral traditions can be incredibly thorough and rigorous about passing their myths on precisely, but they have the option of changing them if they need to – for one of the reasons we've just looked at, for example. Once you've written something down, however, it's much harder to change it.

How myths spread

When cultures with different mythologies mix, their mythologies tend to influence each other. This may be accidental or deliberate. In the accidental version, the people simply swap stories along with the goods or skills that they trade. When one culture comes across a story it likes, and if the story contains elements that either fit in well with its own existing myths, or explain something that they previously had no satisfactory explanation for, they will often 'borrow' it, and incorporate it into their own mythology. For example, the Vikings' end of the world myth almost certainly borrowed elements from the Christian version of the end of the world – virtually everyone the Vikings either conquered or traded with in Europe was Christian.

Sometimes myths are combined more deliberately. When the Romans conquered a new region they knew they couldn't eliminate the local myths. So they created hybrid myths that merged Roman mythology with the indigenous beliefs, and identified local gods with Roman ones. When the Roman empire collapsed, these conquered people were left with a new version of their mythology that was partly Roman. The Christians also did this, so that most Christian festivals happen at a time when there was already a festival. For example,

Lammas comes at the same time as Lughnasadh, the Celtic festival of the god Lugh.

The other example of myths spreading is when tribes conquer new lands. Their mythology may then develop separately from that of the region where they originated, but the shared roots will usually be evident. The Vedic people who settled in north-west India in about 1550 BC came from Persia. Although their contact with the Persians was minimal for a long time after that, there are a number of shared deities, such as Mitra, who was a sun god. He also continued to be worshipped in Persia, under the name Mithras. (He was adopted from Persia 1,500 years or so later by the Romans, who built a cult around his worship.)

Most of the mythologies covered in the following chapters interrelate. The Egyptians influenced the Greeks, the Indians influenced the Chinese, the Celts influenced the Vikings and so on. The time chart illustrated gives you an overview of which of these mythologies were around simultaneously, and had the opportunity to influence each other. Some of the myths may have travelled a long way. The Japanese have one myth (Izanagi and Izanami, see page 113) which is incredibly similar to one of the Greek myths. This is by no means as implausible a link as it may seem at first. The Greeks traded with the Chinese along the Silk Route, and the Chinese heavily influenced the Japanese mythology. It's quite possible that this myth – which is, after all, an extremely good story – could have travelled from the Mediterranean to the Far East.

—— Types of god, types of myth ——

As we have seen, the gods often grow out of fetishes which have particular purposes. A tribe might have a hunting fetish, a rain fetish and so on. The successful fetishes inspire an awe about them that can develop into worship. After a while, people start to do deals with the spirit that resides in the fetish object. One North American tribe, for example, has a hunting fetish which it invokes to give the hunter a share of its courage before the hunt begins. When the hunter is successful, he smears the blood of the animal he has killed on the fetish, to reward it with a taste of the kill that it has helped to provide. This kind of ritual, which usually starts very simply, can become quite complex after a time.

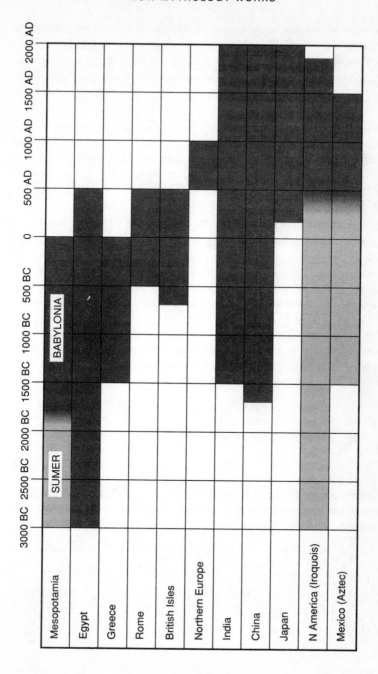

The next stage that these emerging mythologies tend to go through involves an extension of this kind of reasoning. If a fetish that has been successful in the past fails to come up with the goods, perhaps the spirit inside it is tired and needs sustenance. So you make it an offering of food or fortifying blood – a sacrifice. Eventually, through worship, ritual and sacrifice, you end up with a god.

These gods often have their own area of responsibility; probably the function that the fetish was associated with. In some polytheistic mythologies you will find certain functions that seem to have several gods associated with them; this could be because there were several original fetishes, each relating to a different aspect of, say, hunting or fertility. Or it might be because two or more clans or tribes have merged, adding their gods to the collective pantheon in the process.

You can see how the types of gods that most often emerge are the ones who have functions that are important. To some extent, these functions vary according to the lifestyle and location of the tribe they belong to. For example, a sea god – who can be invoked to keep the waters calm and safe – will be far more important to a tribe that lives on the coast than to one that lives far inland. As another illustration of this, the early Indian settlers needed a god who could help them cope with the arid conditions of their new country. This is very possibly why they demoted their chief god and replaced him with a rain god – to fulfil one of their most vital needs.

The two principal types of lifestyle in early cultures are hunting and agricultural farming. These have different needs because crop farmers have to settle in one place, while hunters tend to be nomadic – they can travel long distances looking for game. Hunting tends to develop, logically, into herding. If you breed your own cattle you don't have to go looking for them; you know where they are from the start. But this is usually still a nomadic existence because the best pastures may be far apart; a good summer pasture may be no use at all in the winter.

If you are a herdsman you are likely to come across other clans, and you will frequently end up having to fight them for territory. This means that you will need a strong, dominant male god. You will also need this god to make it rain, so that the grass will grow to feed your cattle and sheep. These tribes usually develop male sky gods as their chief god.

If, on the other hand, you are settled and farming the same area of land every year, you are unlikely to encounter many other tribes. So fighting is not that crucial. What is important, however, is that your crops are 'born' every spring from the earth, and nurtured through the year until they are ready to be harvested. These functions are maternal, and these primitive cultures tend to develop mother-earth goddesses to lead their pantheon who, not surprisingly, have a responsibility for fertility.

Gradually other important gods develop; there are certain types that occur regularly, and often influence later cultures. Popular deities will be borrowed frequently so that you can trace certain deities through several mythologies.

Sky gods are often the chief gods in early pantheons, although they may be deposed later. The early Indian Dyaus derived from the same god as the Greek Zeus and the Roman Jupiter.

Creator gods are often sky gods as well, like the Aztec Tonacatecutli. However, in many mythologies you find that the creator god is very primal in nature, often having little personality, and plays little part in the main body of myths. Sometimes he is even said to have died or gone to live in heaven after completing the creation, like the Chinese Pan Gu. This usually suggests that this god is part of an earlier mythology that has been superseded.

The sun god is often the creator god, since all life was perceived to come from the sun. He is rarely the sun itself, except in a few primitive mythologies; he is more often a god whose home is the sun, like Ra in Egyptian mythology.

Thunder gods are significant in many mythologies, and are often the chief god. For people who lived in mountainous regions, especially, thunder was terrifying and powerful; it was often the thunder god who wielded the lightning. Zeus was a god of thunder, who would have influenced the Viking Thor.

Rain gods are important to both herdsmen and farmers, since their livelihoods depend on the rain. Rain gods are especially important in regions where drought is a threat such as Mexico, where Tlaloc was the rain god. Many sky gods also control the rain, such as Indra, and so do thunder gods such as Zeus.

Fertility gods are often the product of rain gods; either the rain god acquires this role as well, or he produces a son who takes responsibility for fertility. The reason, of course, is that the rain is an essential ingredient in ripening the crops. Gods whose functions incorporate both the rain and fertility include the early Indian Varuna. The job of looking after fertility more often goes to a goddess, but there are plenty of examples of male fertility gods as well, such as Frey (Viking) and Osiris (Egyptian).

Gods of war were important as we have already seen, and were often associated with thunder because of the noise and terror of it. Thor was the god of war as well as of thunder, as was the Babylonian Enlil.

Fire gods tend to be associated with the sun. Later on they may become domestic gods of the hearth, or metalsmiths, using fire for smelting and forging – such as the Greek Hephaestus, the Roman Vulcan or the Norse Thor. Metalworking was only developed relatively late, however, so these gods would likewise have developed later.

Sea gods are, at least in the early stages, almost invariably represented with the tail of a fish – a reflection of their totemic beginnings (and presumably the origin of mermaids and mermen). The Babylonian Ea developed into the Greek Poseidon and the Roman Neptune.

Moon gods were generally female, but not always. Two notable exceptions are the Egyptian Thoth, who was associated with the moon, and the Babylonian god Sin, who derived from the Sumerian Nanna.

Mother goddesses are often dominant in early pantheons. Later they may be married off to the sky god to create a family. The Indian goddess Maha Devi is an example of this. The early Mesopotamian mother goddess Inana developed into the Babylonian Ishtar, the Syrian Astarte, and the Egyptian Isis who was also worshipped by the Greeks and Romans. There is a strong argument that she also influenced, via the Romans, the character of the Christian Virgin Mary.

Fertility goddesses may be separate, or become separated from, the mother goddess. Those that are separate are usually associated with corn or crops. The Phrygian goddess Cybele was both a mother goddess and a fertility goddess; she influenced the Greek Demeter, who was a fertility goddess specifically associated with crops, who developed into the Roman Ceres.

Moon goddesses often develop from a perceived relationship between the moon and fertility. Not only do the crops grow with the seasons, which change with the moon, but the moon also appears to become 'pregnant' and then wane in a regular cycle. Moon deities are usually female because of the obvious connection between the moon's monthly cycle and women's menstrual cycle. Mother goddesses are, therefore, often associated with the moon; examples of this include Inana, Ishtar, Astarte, Isis, and the Virgin Mary, who was often depicted in medieval times with a crescent moon at her feet.

Goddesses of love are a later development, but they tend to develop from fertility goddesses for obvious reasons. Once you apply the fertility to people as well as to crops, you can't really achieve it without sex. Just as the fertility aspect of the mother goddess can generate a fertility goddess, so the fertility goddess can evolve into – or give birth to – both goddesses of the crops and goddesses of love. Ishtar, being both a mother goddess and a fertility goddess, not only influenced a line of mother goddesses but also a string of love goddesses, such as the Greek Aphrodite and the Celtic Freya.

Goddesses of death often come later, but again it's worth mentioning them here since they are often a development of fertility goddesses. The logic behind this is that the crops die and go underground every year, so their goddess goes with them. Examples of this kind of goddess of death include the Babylonian Erishkigal, who is the sister of Ishtar (for sister read 'dark side' or alter ego), the Greek Persephone and the Celtic Rhiannon.

There is one other category of deities that you quite often come across; these are deities that have a special responsibility for humans. They are often – but by no means always – credited with having created them, and they often act or intercede on behalf of humans when other gods cause suffering. Prometheus for example, in Greek myth, stole fire from Zeus to give to the men he had created. And Nü Gua, in China, mended the world when the water god brought the sky down. These gods seem to be either the original totem of the tribe who continues to take an extra special interest or, as in the case of Indra, a genuine historical, human figure who has been reinterpreted as a god.

Symbolism in myths

This is a huge topic, and one that it is impossible to cover in detail here. However, it is possible to look at the principles behind it; then you can start to recognise where symbolism is playing a part in myths.

Mythologies – especially the more complex mythologies – are littered with symbolic references and objects. They are a kind of shorthand which, if you can interpret it, gives you a clue to some deeper meaning behind the myth. To give you a simple example, the presence of a physical bridge in a myth implies a spiritual or mental divide that must be crossed. It signifies a change from one state to another for whoever crosses it (frequently from the state of life to the state of death); often it signifies a link between the known and the unknown. It can also suggest danger, since the bridge is often the narrowest and most risky part of the path. The Norse land of the dead, Niflheim, is separated from the land of the gods, Asgard, by a bridge.

Here's another example: in China, peaches are a symbol of immortality. This symbolism has also been borrowed by the Japanese. In the Japanese myth of Izanagi and Izanami (see page 113), Izanagi visits the underworld. He is chased out of it by the 'hags of hell', but manages to beat them back by pelting them with peaches. This sounds rather implausible, but it makes more sense when you realise that the peaches are just a symbol of the fact that Izanagi has the force and power of the lifeblood in him, and is taunting the hags, who are not even alive.

Once you start to look for the symbolism in myths it becomes easy to recognise. Some of it is fairly obvious to begin with; cords and ropes symbolise mental, social or spiritual bonds, for instance, and weaving symbolises creation and life (the Japanese chief deity, the sun goddess Amaterasu, weaves the other gods' clothes). It's quite simple to spot the symbols, although you may have to look up the meanings of some of them.

Classifying myths

There are certain recurrent themes in myth, which means that an awful lot of them can be classified into groups, such as creation myths; most cultures have some kind of story that answers the question 'How did the world begin?' Listed below are the most important classes of myth.

- **Creation myths** vary, but broadly speaking they all start with nothing, or with some kind of primeval water or darkness. Out of this a god (or occasionally two or three gods) creates himself, and then kicks off the process of creating more gods, and an ordered universe. It's hard to see how early people could have come up with much else by way of an explanation really. They're all variations on 'before there was something... there was nothing'. What is more interesting is the differences between them; this tells you far more about the beliefs of the people who created the myth. Some, such as the Chinese story, include a duality so that right from the start there is always a balance of yin and yang, dark and light. This idea runs right through Chinese philosophy and religion. Other myths, such as the Babylonian and Norse versions, include a god who dies after creating the universe, as a kind of sacrifice. Many mythologies also include a cyclical element: the universe will be destroyed and recreated several times, or even indefinitely. This applies in the Aztec creation story, for example, and in the Hindu version. In the case of the Hindu myth, this reflects their belief that humans, too, will be reincarnated indefinitely.
- **Myths of the origin of humans** explain how the first people were formed by the gods. Sometimes they are moulded from clay or carved from wood, but most often they are created from some part of the god's body: the tears, blood, bones, sweat or even the voice or 'word' of the god. There are a few other versions in which, for example, people arrive after falling out of the sky. In a number of myths man and woman are created separately. In Greek myth woman was created later to bring trouble to the world; the Biblical story of the garden of Eden is not dissimilar.
- **Myths of the cosmos** explain the existence and movement of the sun, moon and stars. The sun is often seen as a boat or a chariot driven across the sky every day by the sun god. The moon changes visibly night by night, and many myths seek to explain this. The early Indian creation myths tell how the moon is being chased round the sky by the demon Rahu, who almost swallows it and then it re-emerges from his mouth. Many myths have similar stories to explain eclipses. The sun and the moon usually represent opposites; almost always one is male and the other (usually the moon) female. Often they are brother and sister. The sun represents day, light,

life, openness and so on, while the moon is associated with night time, darkness, death and secrecy, often in the form of magic or sorcery. Stars, or more specifically constellations, are seen as characters by cultures around the world. Even the most primitive societies seem to have played join-the-dots and come up with identities for groups of stars. They are often believed to be ancestors or gods, and there is a common belief that good people become stars when they die.

- **Flood myths** are common around the world, and may well be mythologised accounts of a real flood in the history of the tribe or nation. Almost invariably all living things drown apart from one person or one family, who sometimes saves other animals as well. It's in the nature of myths, as with all stories, to exaggerate; so if in reality many people drowned, it's likely that the myth would relate that all but one or two had died ('the waters were *this* big!'). In mythologies which have acquired a moral dimension, the flood is put down to the gods punishing mortals for their sins.

- **End of the world myths** are less common than creation myths, but many exist. As well as the creation-destruction-recreation cycles, some mythologies tell of an original creation and a final destruction, often followed by a new and heavenly world. The two best known examples of this are the Norse story of the 'twilight of the gods' and the Christian story of the second coming.

- **Myths of the underworld** usually belong to mythologies that have no belief in judgement after death, although the underworld may well have a social hierarchy similar to the earthly one, so that kings and nobles go to a better place than common people. Sometimes warriors, too, are singled out for special treatment. The underworld that everyone else is consigned to at death is usually a dimly lit, drab place, peopled by shadows, where nothing ever seems to happen. Most cultures locate their underworld somewhere to the west of their lands, since it is the place where the sun goes at night. And the gods often live near to the underworld – again, the sun god spends the night among his fellow deities. Broadly speaking, cultures site their gods and their underworld according to what is on their western horizon, except for some of the mythologies which identify the gods with the stars. Other than these, tribes living near a western sea-coast locate the worlds of the gods below the sea, or on an island just beyond the horizon (like the Irish). Tribes and peoples living to the east of deserts and plains usually believe the gods live in the sky (as in some of the

Egyptian cults), and people with mountains to the west tend to place the gods there (like the Greek Mount Olympus). The under-world, though nearby, is underground since that is where dead bodies – and dead crops – go.

- **Myths of a descent to the underworld**. The underworld is usually reached by travelling along a long and dangerous path (symbolising the transition from life to death). It is almost never entered by people who are still alive, but occasionally a hero or a god will attempt it. Sometimes these myths are part of a search for the secret of immortality, but most often they are part of a fertility myth which explains why the crops disappear underground for part of the year before the new shoots appear. There are two variations on underworld myths worth mentioning. One is the 'food of the dead' motif, in which anyone who eats the food of the under-world while they are there forfeits any chance they may have had of getting out again. The other variation is the group of myths that contain what is known as a dying-and-rising god. These fertility gods actually die (rather than merely visit the underworld) and are reborn, symbolising the cycle of the crop seasons. Dying-and-rising gods include Osiris in Egyptian myth, Attis (Phrygia), Baldur (Norse) and of course Christ.

- **Myths of heaven and hell** tend to be part of mythologies with some kind of morality and a belief that at death, the soul is judged. Since mythologies grow from some variation on the belief that everything has a spirit, it is hardly surprising that almost all mythologies believe that humans have a spirit that outlives their body. Hell is often an exaggerated version of whatever the people fear most: in the far north it tends to be incredibly cold, while in hotter climates it is a place of burning heat.

- **Hero myths** give some kind of example for ideal behaviour, usual-ly glorifying courage and endurance. Examples of heroes include the Greek Hercules, the Celtic Finn mac Cumhal and Cuchulainn, and the Chinese hero Yu the Great.

- **Fire myths**. Fire can be the greatest friend and the most danger-ous enemy, and the two types of fire myth demonstrate this. In the fire-stealing myths, someone (usually a supernatural bird of some kind) steals fire from heaven and gives it to mankind. There is a lot of evidence to suggest that Prometheus, who performs this task in Greek mythology, was derived from a bird totem.

- **Dismemberment myths** usually involve the dismembered body of a god being scattered widely and the pieces subsequently being gathered up again. This happens to Osiris, for example. The victims are fertility gods, and the myths probably recall the custom of dismembering the bodies of sacrificed animals or humans and burying the pieces in the fields as an offering to the gods to help the crops to grow. The bones of the dead were commonly preserved, in all sorts of cultures, in case the person who had died needed them again. When the dismemberment includes castration, this symbolises that the god's supremacy is at an end. When the Greek Kronos deposes his father Uranus, he castrates him.

2

MIDDLE EASTERN MYTHOLOGY

Babylonia

Ten thousand years ago, the first farmers began to work the fertile land between the rivers Tigris and Euphrates, which flow into the northern end of what we now call the Persian Gulf. The word Mesopotamia means 'between rivers'. Once people began to farm, they could settle in one place in a way the nomadic hunting tribes could not, and could generate enough food to feed larger numbers of people than before.

Mesopotamia is known as 'the cradle of civilisation': soon the people began to build towns and even cities, and to develop a more complex social structure. Surplus food meant that they could begin to trade with their neighbours, and the free time they could now spare gave them the chance to invent tools and techniques to improve their standard of living still further. They developed calendars, money, and weights and measures. By about 3000 BC they had started to keep track of their trade by pressing reeds into wet clay which, when dry, formed a permanent record. This was the world's first writing, known as cuneiform (after the distinctive wedge-shaped marks made by the reeds).

The first myths recorded by these people were written down in 2500 BC, and are the earliest recorded literature in the world. The Mesopotamian culture flourished for around 5,000 years, and during that time its myths developed, of course. So did its culture. The first great civilisation of the region was the group of city-states of the Sumerians. These people settled in Sumer around 5000 – 4000 BC.

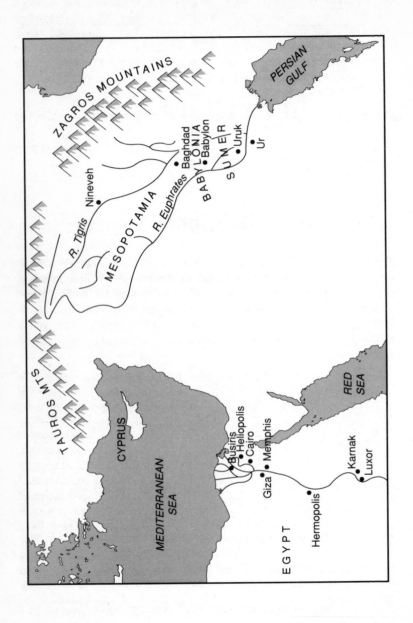

The Sumerians were conquered in 2300 BC and, after a few hundred years of disputes and sporadic warfare, the Babylonians emerged as the next great culture of the region, surviving for around 2,000 years. The Sumerians and Babylonians shared many of the same gods, but several of them took on new roles under the influence of the Babylonians, and there was a shift in the nature of the pantheon. The key differences were that:

- the Sumerian pantheon was essentially matriarchal, while the Babylonians developed a male-dominated religion.
- the Sumerian gods had been regarded as spirits of the natural phenomena they represented – the land, the water, the sky. The Babylonians gave them functions; they actually did things, rather than simply existing.

The mythic systems of Sumer and Babylonia influenced those of other cultures. There was a good deal of cross-fertilisation between Mesopotamian and Egyptian beliefs, and many of these myths were incorporated, adapted or borrowed by the Hebrew tradition (whose followers had spread from Mesopotamia), the classical Greeks and, through them, the religions of northern and western Europe and the Far East.

The purpose of the myths

At the time of Mesopotamian civilisation, many of the natural phenomena that we understand today were still far from being explained scientifically. But the people of the time were no less keen to understand them. So they developed myths to explain them. They believed that the great forces of nature – the sky, the water and so on – caused certain things to happen. This had another advantage, too: it meant that they could control the elements that had so much influence over their lives. For example, they practised astrology and believed that solar and lunar eclipses were provided as an omen that foreshadowed the death of the monarch. As a result, they had developed a way of saving the king when this happened: he would abdicate for a fixed period of 100 days, and a substitute ruler would be put in his place. When the 100 days were up the substitute would be executed (fulfilling the requirement for the monarch to die), and the true monarch would return to his throne.

Many other rituals and practices were developed like this, so that religion played a huge part in the lives of the Babylonians. They weren't all such major events as the threat of the king's death, of course. There were many everyday rituals that people of every rank would practise to placate, satisfy or impress the gods – gods who must exist, because how else could you explain the changing seasons, the floods and so on? As a result of this, the people lived what we would probably consider to be very superstitious lives. They carried amulets and charms, made sacrifices and offered prayers to persuade their deities to bring the rain, protect their families, or do whatever else they believed their gods had power to influence.

Some of the Babylonian myths fall into a different category: they were mythical accounts of events or people from their history. Some of these were simply legends, but many qualify as myths because they were incorporated into the belief system. The great flood myth, for example (see page 29), is a racial memory of an actual flood. There were several of these during Mesopotamia's history, but the worst was around 4000 BC and buried the city of Ur in 3 metres of mud and silt. This is almost certainly the same flood that is recounted in the Old Testament, since the Hebrew people originated in Mesopotamia and shared a common ancient history with the Babylonians.

The Epic of Gilgamesh (page 30) was actually written for a real life character, king Gilgamesh of Uruk, in around 2700 BC. But it passed into mythology because the fictional Gilgamesh was a semi-divine character, who met with gods on his journey. It's a myth about the natural human fear of death, and the search for immortality. The Babylonians did not believe in an afterlife, and Gilgamesh's search is fruitless. He finally has to learn that fame is the only immortality, and that he must learn to value life, as there is nothing else.

There was probably another, more basic purpose that the myths also served. Almost half of Babylonian land was owned by the temples (a reputed 1,179 of them), which were therefore hugely wealthy and powerful. They had an easy method of controlling the people: they terrified them with stories of evil spirits which could be deflected only by doing as the priests dictated.

Gods and goddesses

The Babylonians had numerous gods and goddesses, and people or families tended to adopt an individual deity to attach themselves to.

Many of these were minor deities, or were important only in one or two places in Babylonia. However, there were certain deities who were universally acknowledged as being important.

These really divide into two groups. There were the early, primordial gods, who had been revered by the Sumerians and who remained a part of the Babylonian pantheon. And there were the later gods whom the Babylonians developed into more clearly defined characters than the Sumerians seem to have done.

There were five key primeval deities who were still important to the Babylonians.

Tiamat began as the great mother goddess, and goddess of salt waters. However in later myths, once Marduk had deposed Anu, she came to represent chaos and became an evil enemy of the gods.

Apsu was Tiamat's consort, and the personification of the Apsu, which was a stretch of sweet water believed to run beneath the earth, from which the springs and rivers flowed.

Mammu was Tiamat and Apsu's first son, and was the god of mists.

Anshar was the son of Tiamat and Apsu, and consort of his sister Kishar. Anshar is supposed to have created Anu, and is associated with heaven.

Kishar, Anshar's sister and consort, was said to have created Nantu, and is associated with earth.

There were dozens of other gods worshipped by the Babylonians, but these were the key players in the myths.

Anu, the sky god, was the ruler of the gods to the Sumerians, but was later deposed by Marduk. Anu was the counterpart of Apsu, taking on his role when Apsu was destroyed.

Antu was Anu's consort, a mother goddess. She took on Tiamat's function when Tiamat was defeated and became evil.

Enlil, god of the air and master of men's fates. He replaced his father, Anu, as king of the gods, and then became assimilated into Marduk by the Babylonians.

Ninlil was Enlil's consort, goddess of the air and of grain.

Ea, the son of Anu, was the god of wisdom and of men's work. He presided over the Apsu, the primeval water beneath the earth.

Damkina was Ea's consort.

Marduk was the son of Ea and Damkina. He was a minor deity to the Sumerians, but when the Babylonians rose to power, they changed the original creation myth to make their local god Marduk the chief deity.

Sin was the moon god, and it was his job to measure time. In later versions of the myths, he is the father of Ishtar, who personified the planet Venus.

Shamash was Sin's son, and was the god of the sun and of justice.

Ishtar was the goddess of love, sex and fertility, and war. She was the daughter of Sin (or sometimes Anu in earlier accounts) and her sacred beast was the lion.

Erishkigal was queen of the underworld and elder sister of Ishtar, or in some versions her darker alter ego.

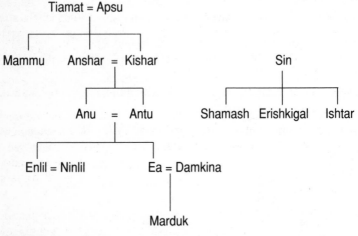

The Babylonian pantheon

The myth of creation

The Babylonian creation myth is usually known as the *Enuma elish*, after its opening words (they mean 'when on high').

At the beginning of time, there is nothing but water and there are just two gods: Tiamat and Apsu. Tiamat rules the salt waters and Apsu rules the sweet, fresh waters. Their first son is Mammu, the mists that swirl around the waters. Then they create Anshar and Kishar; Anshar is the male element and personified the sky, and Kishar, the female element, becomes the earth.

Anshar and Kishar produce children and grandchildren and, before long, there are so many gods and goddesses in the house of the gods that Apsu can't stand it any longer. So he confronts Tiamat, telling her that if the gods don't keep the noise down he will have no choice but to kill them all. Tiamat is furious, and refuses to countenance this, saying that she can't bear the noise either, but Apsu's solution to it would be evil.

Mammu, on the other hand, is on Apsu's side. The two of them plot to put an end to the other gods so they can have some peace. But Ea, the wisest god, gets wind of this plot, and uses his magic powers to put Apsu and Mammu into a deep sleep. Once they are soundly asleep he kills them, and then takes Apsu's place as king of the gods. Ea and his consort, Damkina, settle in Apsu's house and Damkina gives birth to Marduk. Ea is so pleased with his son that he makes him a double god, stronger and better than any other god. He gives him four eyes and four ears, so he can see and hear everything, and every time Marduk opens his mouth, fire blazes from it.

Meanwhile, Tiamat is unhappy at the death of Apsu and, encouraged by a faction of gods who are unhappy with Ea, decides to avenge him. So she creates an army of serpents, terrible dragons, scorpion men, wild dogs and other monsters. She appoints the god Kingu as leader of her army, and gives him the Tablet of Destinies, which confers supreme power on him.

When Ea hears about Tiamat's battle plans, he consults his grandfather, Anshar. Anshar agrees that someone must fight and defeat Tiamat. He tries to persuade Anu to march against her, but he hasn't got the nerve to face her. Ea, likewise, backs off at the thought of the confrontation. Finally they send for Marduk, who shows no fear and is entirely confident that he can defeat Tiamat. But he does lay down one condition. If he wins, the other gods must agree to make him king of the gods.

Anshar calls a great conference of the gods, and they agree to hold a banquet for Marduk where they can test his powers to see if he deserves to become supreme god. At the banquet, they give him a garment and ask him to prove his power by making it disappear and then reappear. He does this successfully, and the gods agree that they are quite happy to have him as their supreme ruler if he defeats Tiamat.

Marduk goes into battle, wielding a terrifying array of weapons that includes lightning and hurricanes, and riding a storm chariot drawn by four beasts called Destroyer, Pitiless, Trampler and Flier. He also takes with him a net with which to catch Tiamat.

Marduk and Tiamat meet in single combat. He throws the net around her, and she opens her mouth to swallow him. But he drives the wind into her mouth so she can't close it, then sends other winds into her body to spread it out and, finally, shoots her with an arrow that splits her down the middle, pierces her heart and kills her.

After his victory, Marduk takes the Tablet of Destinies from Kingu and then throws him and the rest of Tiamat's monsters into the infernal regions. He slices Tiamat's body in half 'like a fish', and creates a roof for the sky out of one half, and the earth from the other half. Then he sets Anu to govern the heavens, Ea to govern the earth, and gives Enlil rulership of the air between the earth and the heavens.

Marduk continues to create order out of the chaos that had reigned until now. He organises the year into months, arranges the stars and directs Sin to shine at night in various phases. He creates Shamash, the sun, and then makes wind, rain and clouds from Tiamat's spittle. He uses her head to make the mountains of the earth, and causes the Tigris and the Euphrates to flow from her eyes. Marduk then peoples the earth, making man out of the blood of Kingu, and tells the people that he has created them to serve the gods.

The gods need never work again, now that Marduk has created man to serve them. But as a last act before they give themselves up to a life of eternal freedom, the gods spend two years building the great temple and ziggurat (the temple enclosure) of Esagila at Babylon, so that they have a home to live in when they visit earth.

The Story of the Flood

The Babylonian flood myth is contained within the *Epic of Gilgamesh*, as a story within a story. It is particularly interesting if you are familiar with the story of Noah's Ark, since the similarities are clear, for reasons we saw earlier.

The gods decide to destroy the human race (for reasons that are never made clear). But Ea is less keen on the idea than his fellow gods, because he pities mankind. So he whispers the plan to a reed hut in the village of Shuruppak. As he has intended, this is overheard by one of the local inhabitants, a man named Ut-napishtim. Ea warns him to pull his house down to build a boat, and save all the living things he can gather by putting them on the boat. Ea tells Ut-napishtim to forget material possessions and concentrate on saving lives.

Ut-napishtim listens to the advice and builds the boat to detailed instructions. Then he loads the boat with gold and silver and the 'seed of all living things'. He takes his family on board, and his cattle, wild animals and birds, and craftsmen. That evening, rain and mud begin to fall, and they lock the doors of the boat. For six days and nights the storm rages so fiercely that even the gods are afraid; the goddess Ishtar even regrets having supported the idea of a deluge in the first place.

Eventually the storm ends, and the boat is left floating on waters that stretch to the horizon. Ut-napishtim is in tears when he sees that 'all mankind is turned into mud'. The boat comes to rest on the summit of Mount Nisir, the only land left above water level. He sends out a dove, which returns, and then a swallow, which also returns. Finally he sends a raven which doesn't return, indicating that the waters are receding and there is dry land at last.

Ut-napishtim makes a huge sacrifice to the gods who decide to make him and his wife immortal like themselves.

The Epic of Gilgamesh

This story is Sumerian, based on the real king Gilgamesh who reigned around 2700 BC. However, it is probably older in origin, and was reworked for Gilgamesh with himself as the hero. The several versions of it that now survive were written down between about 2000 BC and 630 BC, so the story survived well into Babylonian times, and was still popular 2,000 years after the real Gilgamesh had died.

This myth bears a striking similarity to the Greek myth of Theseus and Pirithous. These two start out as enemies but become close friends. Theseus is distraught when his friend becomes trapped for ever in the underworld. The Greeks would have known the story of Gilgamesh, and could easily have borrowed from it. It contains a good deal of symbolism; for example, sleep represents death, and the snake symbolises rebirth.

At the start of the epic Gilgamesh, the semi-divine but mortal son of a goddess is a young and energetic king of Uruk. So energetic, in fact, that he wears everyone else out. He exhausts all the young men of Uruk by making them build the city walls and the temple all day long, and at night he tires out all the beautiful young women of the city. Not only that, but he shows no respect for tradition and interferes constantly in everyone's lives.

In desperation, the people finally invoke the gods to find a solution to the problem of Gilgamesh's behaviour. The god Anu summons Ninku, who had created Gilgamesh in the first place, and tells her that she must create another man to rival him. This rival must be as strong and as energetic as Gilgamesh, so that he will keep the king occupied and he will leave his people in peace.

So Ninku creates Enkidu, who is wild and primitive. He lives with the animals, eats grass and goes naked. Gilgamesh tries to trap this rival, who is reputed to be as strong as he is. But first he has to tame him. So he sends a harlot to seduce Enkidu; after a week with her the animals reject Enkidu, because he has lost his innocence and become human. He can no longer live in the wild so, persuaded by the harlot, he goes to live in Uruk.

Enkidu learns of Gilgamesh's strength and relishes the prospect of challenging him. He finds an opportunity to do this when he blocks Gilgamesh's way, and the king responds by wrestling him. After a long and equally matched fight, Gilgamesh finally falls to one knee. But the two men have such admiration for each other's strength that instead of being enemies, they become firm friends.

One day Gilgamesh finds his friend Enkidu in tears, because he knows that the comforts of city life are taking the edge off his strength, and he is no longer as fit as he used to be when he lived with the animals. Gilgamesh has a solution to cheer him up. He suggests that they head off to the pine forest and kill the monstrous giant Humbaba, who spreads flood, fire and death. This seems to Enkidu to be an excellent way of regaining his old strength and sharpness, so they set off together.

They reach Humbaba, who is so huge that they seem to have no chance against him. However, the gods intervene and help them to capture the giant, and Gilgamesh and Enkidu finish him off together.

Back in Uruk, they clean up and put on their best robes. When the love goddess Ishtar sees Gilgamesh looking so glamorous she throws herself at him and begs him to marry her. But Gilgamesh isn't a fool. He points out to Ishtar that she has ended up torturing and killing every lover she has ever had, so the offer isn't really as tempting as she would have him believe. He becomes carried away with his argument, and begins to insult Ishtar, telling her that she is like a back door that doesn't keep out the storm, or a headdress that doesn't cover the head.

Ishtar is furious at being scorned and insulted, and she goes to the god Anu and asks him to give her the Bull of Heaven so that she can use it to kill Gilgamesh. Anu tries to suggest that Ishtar started the argument with Gilgamesh herself, but Ishtar threatens that if Anu doesn't agree to her request she will cause the dead to rise up and eat the living so that they outnumber them. Eventually, Anu gives in and lets her take the Bull of Heaven.

Ishtar leads the Bull into Uruk. When it snorts, a huge pit opens up into which 200 young men of Uruk fall and die. At the second snort, another 200 go the same way. Finally, at the third snort, Enkidu throws himself at the Bull. It lashes out with its tail, but Gilgamesh joins in the fight and, between them, the two heroes kill the Bull.

They ride in triumph through Uruk, but Ishtar climbs on the city walls and curses Gilgamesh for insulting her by killing the Bull.

Unfortunately for Gilgamesh and Enkidu, the Bull of Heaven is the personification of the will of the gods. Having killed it, they have in effect opposed the will of the gods and they have to be punished for it. The gods gather to discuss this, and agree that Enkidu must die, and that Gilgamesh's punishment will be to live deprived of his friend.

The next morning Enkidu falls ill, and within a few days he is dead. Gilgamesh is heartbroken, and Enkidu's death brings home to him his own mortality and fear of death. He orders great statues of Enkidu to be made from precious stones and metals, he wanders the wilderness that Enkidu came from, and he refuses to bury his friend until maggots start to crawl out of Enkidu's body. After the great funeral, Gilgamesh becomes obsessed with finding the secret of immortality, and he sets off to search for it.

He decides to visit his ancestor Ut-napishtim, who gained immortality as a reward for surviving the great flood. The journey is dangerous, and he meets all sorts of hazards on the way. Finally he reaches Ut-napishtim, who tells him his story. Gilgamesh asks how he can achieve immortality, and Ut-napishtim suggests he begin with a trial. He advises him to stay awake for six days and nights, the length of time that the flood lasted.

Gilgamesh sits down to begin his ordeal, and instantly sleep comes over him. He wakes up seven days later and won't believe that he has slept for a week until he sees the seven loaves of bread by his head that have been piling up daily while he has been asleep, some of which are starting to go mouldy. Ut-napishtim and his wife reflect that a hero who cannot even conquer sleep is hardly likely to defeat death. Gilgamesh is deeply disappointed, but Ut-napishtim is persuaded by his wife to help him once more. So Ut-napishtim shows Gilgamesh a magical plant of rejuvenation. He explains that it will not make him live forever, but it will keep him young and strong until the day he dies. The plant grows at the bottom of the sea. Gilgamesh manages to dive down and pick the plant, and then heads back to Uruk.

On the way, he stops to wash in a pool. He removes his clothes and leaves them in a pile at the side of the pool, and carefully puts the magical plant on top of the pile. But a snake smells the sweetly scented plant, slithers out of the water and carries the plant off in its mouth. As it disappears it sheds its skin, emerging younger and fresher.

Gilgamesh finally realises that he will never achieve immortality, and so he resigns himself to the prospect of death and returns to Uruk. As he approaches the city, he reflects on his achievement in building the city walls, and the great temple of Anu and Ishtar. He realises that although he has to die in the end, his name can live forever through his great works. He has his story written on stone tablets and sets them on the walls of Uruk so his people can read them and remember him.

Gilgamesh reigns as a wiser and popular king after this, but his death is not recorded since the story claims to be commissioned by him during his lifetime.

Egypt

The initial impression of Egyptian mythology is that it's extremely complicated. This is because there isn't really one single mythology, but a number of interrelated mythologies. The thing to bear in mind is that beliefs were localised, so each city would have its own god whom the citizens would believe to be the supreme creator god. And not only did beliefs vary from place to place, they also changed over time. A minor deity in early Egyptian civilisation could become a great god, with a huge cult centre, a few centuries later.

Like the Mesopotamians, the early Egyptians first began to settle and farm the land around the Nile valley in about 3000 BC. Before this, they had lived in hunting tribes, and each tribe had its own animistic god; in other words, they believed that every animal and object had its own divine spirit. So their tribal god would be a particular bird, or an animal, or a thunderbolt. As people began to settle and farm the land, these tribes formed towns and cities, and each of their gods would become the local god of that area. Gradually these gods became humanised, although they often retained the head of the animal in whose form they had first been revered.

These gods may have been worshipped alone to begin with, but family was hugely important to the early Egyptians, so their gods had to have families too. Often the female consort they provided became the more senior deity after a time. These two were usually provided with a son, who was frequently the local ruler – a divine god-king in human form. As well as these local gods, the Egyptians also worshipped the great nature gods: the sky, the earth, the sun, the moon and so on. And, of course, the River Nile.

The Egyptians began to write down the myths, in the hieroglyphic text that they had developed, in around 2000 BC, about 500 years after the Mesopotamians. Both cultures depended heavily on the rivers whose alluvial plains they farmed, and they worshipped these rivers. Both believed that natural disasters such as flood and famine were sent by the gods. However, the Nile was a predictable, safe river – the floods were regular and the Egyptians could plan around them. The Tigris and Euphrates, on the other hand, were fierce, dangerous and unpredictable. Not only could they flood without warning, washing away entire towns, but they often changed their courses in the process, so that a town that was once on the banks of the river was suddenly miles from it. As a result of this difference in their lifestyles caused by the rivers they depended on, the Egyptian gods were more predictable and benevolent than the gods of the Mesopotamians.

After a time, several great cult centres emerged in Egypt, each with their own supreme god. These included:

● Hermopolis, the centre of the cult of Thoth
● Heliopolis, where they worshipped Ra
● Memphis, the cult centre of Ptah
● Busiris, where they followed the cult of Osiris
● Karnak, the centre of the cult of Amun.

Many of the most important deities would have been known and worshipped across Egypt, but their relative seniority would have varied from region to region. The total number of deities in the Nile valley was vast: 740 are listed in the tomb of one Pharaoh.

The Egyptians were quite isolated economically, but there was some trade with the people of Mesopotamia and, later on, with other Mediterranean cultures. So the Egyptian myths were sometimes borrowed from the Mesopotamians, and they went on to influence the Greeks and the Romans considerably. Egyptian culture lasted until about 400 AD, around 3,500 years, although from 332 BC Egypt was ruled by the Greeks and then the Romans. In this time, of course, the mythology changed a great deal.

The purpose of the myths

Like the Babylonians, the Egyptians developed myths to explain natural phenomena. So most of their myths are some form of explanation of the way the world functions. The myth of Ra and Apep, for example (see page 41), explains the cycle of day and night, and is an example of the good versus evil motif.

Unlike the Babylonians, however, the Egyptians believed in the existence of the soul which could achieve life after death. This belief largely stemmed from (or developed alongside) the myth of Osiris, which is a classic myth of death (see page 42). Since Osiris was part human, it followed that if he could be reborn, so could they.

Once the Egyptians began to believe in the soul they developed a greater respect for human life and, among other developments, gave up cannibalism. After a time, they began to believe that the key to achieving this immortality was to lead a good life. Many cultures never really made this connection; to the Babylonians the only way to impress the gods was to sacrifice or pray to them. The gods didn't care how their people behaved the rest of the time. And why should the Babylonian people care? So long as they could dissuade the gods from playing cruel tricks on them, there was no reason to follow any particular form of behaviour. There wasn't the promise of an afterlife to tempt them.

Having made this moral distinction between good and evil behaviour, the Egyptians' gods came to reflect this too. There were good gods and evil gods, something the Mesopotamians had never distinguished between.

The Egyptians did, however, share with the Babylonians the belief that in early times there had been chaos, and that the gods had brought order to it. The pharaoh, divine himself, was also the chief priest. Below him were all the other priests, his assistants. Their function was to maintain order, and to perform religious ceremonies to keep the world functioning correctly – to make sure the sun still rose every day, the waters of the Nile continued to flow, and so on. It's easy to see from this how the pharaoh, in fact, controlled a huge administrative bureaucracy, and religion would have been used to 'persuade' the people to do as he wished. This is a far simpler method of control to use once you have the threat of depriving people of their immortality.

The gods and goddesses

Although an impressive number of Egyptian texts survive, they still leave huge gaps in many of the stories. Our best information comes from the Greeks, who wrote several accounts of Egyptian beliefs from about the first century BC. Many of these appear to be surprisingly unbiased and accurate (reports by observers from foreign cultures are notoriously unreliable as a rule); nevertheless, it means that the fullest accounts we have date from comparatively recently in ancient Egyptian culture.

As with the Mesopotamian myths, it is quite easy to recognise many of the earliest gods; they tend to represent aspects of nature such as earth, air and sky. They also play a smaller part in the stories as a rule: they simply exist, where the later gods are more active and more prone to interfere in human lives.

The Egyptians had a dualistic view of things: they believed that a whole was created from two opposites, so that you must have both good and evil, dark and light, order and chaos. This view is evident in their pantheon, which has many pairs of gods representing earth and sky, for example, or sun and moon.

As people traded and moved around Egypt as time went on, the most important gods became more widely recognised. The summary below lists the most important of the Egyptian deities. However, there were still local differences, and changes over time, so you'll often find that more than one deity has the same function (there are several sky gods, for example). These overlapping gods would rarely have been worshipped in the same place at the same time; when this did happen, they tended to become merged together.

Atum, the original creator god, was worshipped at Heliopolis. When Ra's cult became dominant, Atum was eventually merged with Ra to become Ra-Atum. The name Atum means 'the all', and signifies that Atum existed before heaven and earth, who were his children. He was a protective god, and it was his role to raise the dead pharaohs up from the pyramids to be transformed into star gods. Atum is associated with many animals, in particular the lion, the bull and the scarab. In his primordial form he is a snake, the form he was expected to take on again at the end of time.

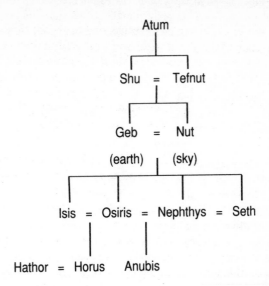

The Egyptian pantheon
This is a version of the family tree of the gods of Heliopolis, one of the most influential cult centres. It is worth including because it can be helpful to see a visual link between a group of about a dozen major gods. However, it is not absolute; you will find certain versions of the myths that do not tally with it entirely. Nevertheless, it is probably the nearest thing in Egyptian mythology to a consistent family group.

Shu was the god of air and sunlight, though not the sun itself. However, he was closely associated with the sun and with Ra. It was Shu's job to separate the sky from the earth by supporting his daughter, the sky god Nut. The Babylonians also had a god of the air between the earth and the sky, Enlil, which indicates that they believed the sky was solid, like the earth. Shu was both brother and husband of Tefnut, and father of Geb (the earth) and Nut.

Tefnut, Shu's sister and wife, was the goddess of moisture and was associated with the moon (in other words she was the 'other half' of Shu). When Ra and Atum merged, Tefnut and Shu became Ra-Atum's eyes, and took the heads of a lioness and a lion.

Geb, another of the older gods, not only represented the earth, he *was* the earth. All vegetation was believed to grow out of his back, so he was often portrayed as being green. When he was in a benevolent mood he was the god of fertility, but he could also be malevolent, imprisoning the dead inside his body. Earthquakes were his laughter. His emblem was a goose, which he often wore on his head. He was the brother and husband of the sky goddess Nut, and father of Osiris, Isis, Seth and Nephthys.

Nut, sister and wife of Geb, formed the sky by bending over the earth, her husband. The sky was her belly, and the stars were sometimes seen as jewels on her robes. She was occasionally portrayed as a cow, so she was sometimes confused with Hathor, with whom the symbol of the cow was most often identified.

Osiris was certainly established in the Egyptian pantheon by 2400 BC so he is a very early god. At first, he embodied the spirit of the vegetation which dies each year with the harvest and is reborn. He came to represent death, resurrection and fertility, and is often depicted as a mummy. He was always a major deity, but he reached the peak of his importance under the Greeks, with a cult centre at Busiris, and also at Alexandria where he was merged with other gods to become Serapis. Osiris is the husband and brother of Isis and the father of Horus.

Isis, wife and sister of Osiris, was the great goddess of fertility and life, who was often symbolised as a cow. She represented all the best parts of women, such as love, loyalty, protection, motherhood and sexuality. She was also clever and skilled in magic. In later times she became even more important than her husband Osiris.

Seth was another of the children of Geb and Nut. Early in Egyptian culture he was the god of chaos and confusion, who brought storms and bad weather. As with the Babylonians, the later gods brought order and controlled chaos, and as the mythology developed Seth came to be seen as downright evil, rather than simply chaotic. He was the patron of the desert and of foreign lands (both of which were seen as enemies), and consequently acquired various foreign goddesses as consorts. One of the most widely recognised of these was the Syrian goddess Astarte (a version of the Babylonians' Ishtar). Seth was married to his sister Nephthys.

Nephthys was lucky enough to be associated with her saintly sister Isis rather than with her evil husband and brother Seth. She was the protector of the dead, and mummy wrappings were thought to represent her hair. In later traditions she was the mother of Anubis from a union with her other brother, Osiris.

Horus, the falcon-headed god, was the son of Isis and Osiris and was thought to take human form in the body of the living pharaoh. He was another sky god; his left eye was the moon and his right eye was the sun. In later times he was frequently merged with Ra (to form Ra-Horakhty).

Anubis was the jackal-headed god of the dead, who supervised the judgement of souls. He was also the god of mummification. It may well be that his association with the jackal grew up from the need to keep corpses away from jackals before burial. Anubis was eventually assimilated into Osiris, who was his father in some versions.

Ra was the sun god, whose cult centre was at Heliopolis. He eventually became widely recognised as the supreme creator god, and merged with many of the other regional creator gods who then took the prefix Ra- ; for example, Ra-Atum. Ra was a hawk-headed god during the day, but in his night-time form he was often depicted with a ram's head. He was sometimes identified with Atum and Atum's family, but when his identity was separate he was said to have several daughters, the most important of whom are listed below.

Maat, often regarded as a daughter of Ra, was the goddess of truth and justice. Her symbol was the ostrich feather, and she was involved in the judgement of the dead. Their hearts were weighed in the scales against her feather of truth – only if the heart was lighter would the soul be rewarded by being allowed to go on to the kingdom of Osiris. Maat also symbolised order, so she was in charge of regulating the seasons and the movement of the stars and so on.

Hathor, another of Ra's daughters, was worshipped as a cow, or a woman with a cow's ears. She was frequently regarded as the wife of Horus. When angry, she sometimes became a lion and, in this form, was one of the 'eyes of Ra'. Hathor was believed to be able to set the destiny of newborn babies, and was commonly associated with the desert (a place all Egyptians feared) and foreign lands. Hathor was often confused with Isis, who also took the cow as her symbol, and was eventually eclipsed by her.

Sekhmet was the lioness-headed daughter of Ra. She often represented the aggressive side of the other female goddesses, but in later times she was associated more specifically with the angry form of her sister, Mut. She was sometimes considered to be the right eye of Horus (the sun).

Bastet was the gentler side of her sister Sekhmet. She was cat-headed and turned into the lioness Sekhmet only when roused. She was often seen as the left eye of Horus, the moon. (The duality of Sekhmet and Bastet is not unlike that of Erishkigal and Ishtar in Babylonian mythology.) Bastet started out as a relatively minor deity, but in later times she was hugely important in her cult centre of Bubastis, where archaeologists have found tombs containing thousands of mummified cats.

Mut, another daughter of Ra, was vulture-headed and was associated with her sister Sekhmet when her mood was aggressive. Occasionally, she was also represented as her sister Bastet, in the guise of a cat. She was consort of Amun, and as such had her own temple at Karnak.

Amun was almost unknown in early Egyptian times, but grew to become one of the most powerful creators and king of the gods. His cult centre was at Karnak, where his temple still survives. He became merged with Ra, as did so many of the creator gods, to become Amun-Ra. He was the husband of Mut.

Ptah was the consort of Sekhmet, whose cult centre was at Memphis. He was often depicted as a mummy. He had originally been the god of craftsmen, but eventually became a creator god, perhaps because of his skill at making things. As a result of these associations he was often considered to be the father of Imhotep, the architect of the first ever pyramid, at Saqqara, who was later deified. By around 750 BC Ptah had been merged with Osiris.

Thoth was the god of writing and knowledge, and hence of secret knowledge and magic. He was also a moon god. It was his job to record the results of the judgement of the dead. He was originally depicted as a baboon, and later he was also represented as an ibis, perhaps because its long, curved beak resembled the crescent moon. Thoth was the guardian of the deceased, and an intermediary or messenger between gods. Occasionally he is seen as the brother of Osiris, but more often he has no family relationship to him, but is Osiris' vizier. He is sometimes associated with Maat, the goddess of truth.

The myth of creation

The Egyptians didn't have a single myth of the creation of the earth. They had several creator gods located in different centres, and each had his own creation story. These early myths were simple and did not consist of narrative storylines, but restricted themselves to explaining the mechanics of creation.

At Memphis, Ptah was said to have created gods and kings out of precious metals (he was the god of crafts). After he had created the first of them, he brought the rest to life by thinking of them in his heart, and then saying their names out loud.

The cult of Thoth at Hermopolis believed that Thoth (god of knowledge and writing) had created everything with the sound of his voice. When he opened his mouth, four pairs of gods and goddesses leapt from it. These eight deities are known as the Ogdoad, and were usually represented as primeval creatures such as frogs and snakes, although they are occasionally depicted as baboons (one of Thoth's forms). They used language to complete the work of creation; by singing and chanting they brought order to the world.

The other principal creation myth was centred around Atum, or Ra-Atum, at Heliopolis. Here, they held that at the beginning of time there had been nothing but Nun, the primordial sea. In the midst of this sea was a spirit which contained the totality of everything: Atum. This spirit created himself using the forces of magic, perception and the divine word. He then produced the first life – his children Shu (air) and Tefnut (moisture) – by a combination of spitting, masturbating and sneezing. These were two opposites, which between them could engender everything else. Shu and Tefnut then produced earth and heaven: Geb and Nut. These two, in turn, produced the deities that are more concerned with humanity: Osiris, Seth, Isis and Nephthys. The first nine gods in the Heliopolitan system are known as the Ennead. The number nine was important to the Egyptians, and crops up frequently. Thoth and the Ogdoad he produced, taken together, also add up to nine gods who between them create all the others.

The myth of Ra and Apep

This is not a story of something that happened once, long ago, but a myth that explains something that happens all the time: the cycle of day and night. It is a myth that deals with the duality of good and evil, night and day.

Every morning, the sun god Ra begins his journey through the sky, sailing in the great solar bark across the twelve regions of Egypt. His all–seeing eye looks down in judgement as he crosses the heavens until, at dusk, his bark reaches the entrance to the underworld. For the next twelve hours, he must sail through the underworld, the land of Osiris, passing through the twelve caverns populated by the righteous dead, who never see daylight except for the hour that Ra spends crossing their cavern.

But Ra's arch-enemy lives in the underworld: the serpent Apep (the Egyptian counterpart of Tiamat, the Mesopotamian goddess of chaos). Every night, Apep attacks Ra, and wrestles with him through the night. In some versions of the myth, Apep tries to stop the bark by drinking all the water beneath it. But eventually Ra, sometimes taking the form of a great cat, defeats Apep by cutting off his head. And every morning, he emerges safely from the underworld to begin his journey again.

Apep occasionally succeeded in swallowing the solar bark – during eclipses – but Ra always managed to defeat him eventually.

The myth of Osiris

The myth of Osiris explains the death and renewal of the crops each year, since Osiris originally represented the crops. He then went on to become the god of fertility, and the god of death and rebirth. There are several variations on the details of this myth, such as precisely how Seth kills Osiris; the version here is one of the most commonly told. This myth also demonstrates the Egyptians' belief that their gods were not immortal, a belief that is often overlooked since the gods could live for so long that the difference often seemed immaterial. However, they did kill off their gods occasionally, especially local gods that had been ousted by another, stronger cult.

According to this myth, Osiris' father Geb abdicates as ruler of Egypt in favour of his son. Osiris civilises his people; he abolishes cannibalism and teaches them agriculture, music and wine making. After a while, he decides it would be a good idea to go and civilise the rest of the world as well. So off he goes, leaving Isis to rule in his absence.

He comes back to find that Isis has ruled extremely wisely. But Seth, his evil brother, is angry at Osiris' return because he is jealous of his power. So he plots to kill his brother. Seth tricks Osiris into getting into a great coffer he has made, and then shuts the lid on him. He seals it, and casts Osiris adrift in the Nile. The coffer is eventually washed up in Byblos (in modern-day Lebanon), where it becomes entangled with the roots of a great cedar tree.

Meanwhile, Isis has been searching constantly for her husband. Eventually she hears of the coffer and brings it back to Egypt, where she hides his body in the marshes until she has made arrangements to bury it. Seth, however, stumbles across the body, and is so angry to find his brother's body still in existence that he dismembers it, scattering the pieces across Egypt.

Isis dutifully searches again for her husband, and finds each piece of his body (as many as forty-two of them in some versions). She cannot find his genitals, however, which are lost for good, so she manufactures an artificial phallus for him. She uses her magical powers to reverse the decay of Osiris' body, and she calls Thoth to help his master by reciting incantations in his pure voice. She asks Anubis to help her by embalming and bandaging Osiris; Osiris becomes the first body ever to be mummified. Isis manages to breathe life into Osiris and, as they are reunited, Horus is conceived.

Having been brought back to life, Osiris could choose to stay on earth. But instead he decides to become the lord of the underworld, where he welcomes the souls of the dead who have lived good lives.

3

EUROPEAN MYTHOLOGY

Greece

Like the Egyptians, the Greeks had hundreds of gods and goddesses, many of whom were only minor or local deities. Their mythology, too, adapted over time. But unlike the Egyptians', it did finally crystallise into a more or less settled structure. One of the reasons for this may well have been that the Greeks developed language, philosophy and the arts further than any other Mediterranean or Middle Eastern culture had before. They wrote stories for sheer entertainment, where other cultures had always had some religious or practical reason for recording their myths.

The Greeks wrote down many of their myths as early as 750 BC; and once something is written down in black and white, it is far less prone to change than when it's being passed on by word of mouth only. The Greeks also managed to create incredibly intricate myths, many of which had plots that wove in and out of each other.

Greece was settled by waves of invaders, from the north and from the east, over a period of about 400 years, up to around 1900 BC. Even after that, it was not a single united country, but a group of states that gradually stabilised into a clear pattern. Greek civilisation flourished from about 1500 BC. It had to absorb other, existing mythologies into it, such as the pagan beliefs that existed there earlier. The great mother goddess, Hera, was a dominant force in earlier pagan mythology, known as pre-Hellenic mythology (after the Greeks' name for their own country: Hellas). The Greek settlers couldn't oust Hera, so they married her to their great sky god Zeus.

Many other pre-Hellenic gods were absorbed into classical Greek mythology, some of whom slotted in better than others – many were still recognised but were left without a clearly defined role. When the Greeks conquered the island of Crete in about 1450 BC, they also took over and adapted the myths of the Minoans who lived there.

The Greeks borrowed a great deal of their mythology from the more ancient cultures around them, including the Babylonians and the Egyptians, particularly after Alexander the Great's conquest of Egypt and the Middle East, and as far as India, around 330 BC.

Like the Egyptians, the Greeks had many gods who were worshipped only locally. But they did have many deities and myths that were recognised right across the Hellenic world. Indeed this was one of the key factors that united this collection of city-states, islands and colonies, and gave them an identity that separated them from the 'barbarians' beyond their borders.

Because of the geography of Greece, the sea was tremendously important to its people, and many of their myths and legends involve stories of the sea. Since trading by sea was vital to them, there are many tales of sea voyages and adventures.

Although Greece finally became a Roman province in 146 BC, its mythology survived since it was absorbed virtually wholesale by the Romans.

The purpose of the myths

Most of the Greek myths are allegorical accounts of events in their distant history, or attempts to explain natural events. The myth of Demeter and Kore (page 51) explains, like the Egyptian myth of Osiris, where the spirit of the corn goes for the months between the harvest and the new shoots appearing again in the spring. The story of Prometheus (page 53) tells how people first discovered fire.

Unlike the Egyptians, the Greeks did not make a strong link between their own behaviour and their religious beliefs. Few of their gods were exclusively good or evil, and they did not set any kind of example for human behaviour. It was only late in Greek civilisation that they developed any idea of a judgement after death based on how they had behaved in life.

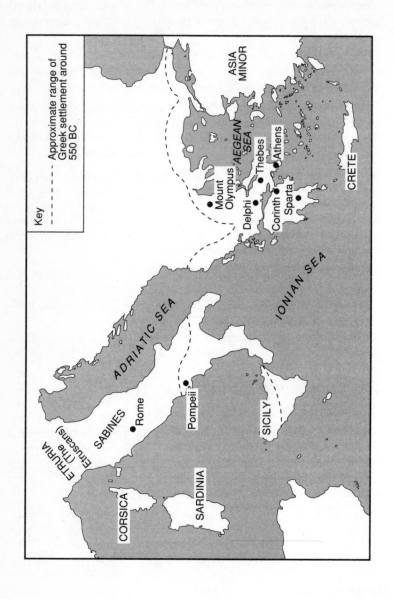

Key

------ Approximate range of
Greek settlement around
550 BC

ASIA MINOR

AEGEAN SEA

Mount Olympus

Delphi

Thebes

Athens

Corinth

Sparta

CRETE

ADRIATIC SEA

IONIAN SEA

Rome

SABINES

Pompeii

SICILY

ETRURIA (The Etruscans)

CORSICA

SARDINIA

The Greeks' lives were full of religious rites, ceremonies and festivals, and every home would have an altar to the household gods. But the Greeks didn't attach any moral or spiritual dimension to this; it was a purely practical expedient. If you kept the gods happy, they might deign to smile on you. In any case, you certainly didn't want to rouse their anger by failing to show them the proper respect.

The Greeks' love of philosophy led them to analyse their own religious beliefs more deeply than other cultures had done. As early as 400 BC Plato was saying that the myths were fictional stories (he was the first person recorded using the word *mythologia*). And in 316 BC a Sicilian philosopher called Euhemerus argued that myths were fictionalised accounts of historical events, and that the gods were real people who had been deified for their heroic behaviour. Nevertheless, while the educated Greeks grew sceptical, the common people continued to recount the stories and to make prayers and sacrifices to their gods.

The gods and goddesses

There are far more gods and goddesses in the Greek pantheon than there is room to list here, but these are the most important. Not all the relationships between them are consistent in every version; this summary gives the most widely accepted version in each case.

Uranus was a sky god, the first ruler of the gods and father of the Titans (the first generation of gods). He was deposed by his son Kronos.

Gaia was the earth mother. She was both mother and consort of Uranus, and gave birth to the twelve Titans.

Rhea was one of the Titans, sister and wife of Kronos and mother of Zeus.

Kronos, the youngest Titan, deposed and replaced his father Uranus, and was in turn deposed by his son Zeus.

Zeus was the sky god and ruler of the gods after defeating his father Kronos.

Hera, Zeus' wife and sister, was the queen of Mount Olympus where the gods lived, and the goddess of marriage and childbirth. She was jealous of Zeus' numerous other lovers and of his illegitimate children.

Poseidon was the brother of Zeus and god of the sea.

Hades, brother of Zeus and Poseidon, was god of the underworld.

Hestia was the sister of Zeus and goddess of the hearth and home. She was one of the Greeks' most popular deities. She was a virgin, claiming to be married to the sacred hearth fire. Virgins were associated with the hearth since it was traditionally the job of the Greek maidens to tend the fire.

Demeter was the sister of Zeus and goddess of the grain and the harvest. She was also, like Gaia, a mother goddess.

Kore, the daughter of Demeter, became Persephone, queen of the underworld.

Helios was the son of a Titan and the god of the sun. He was later replaced by Apollo.

Selene was the sister of Helios and was originally the goddess of the moon. She was subsequently replaced by Artemis.

Eos, sister of Helios and Selene, was goddess of the dawn.

Atlas was the son of a Titan and very strong. For this reason he was forced by Zeus to hold up the sky for ever as a punishment for not joining Zeus in his battle against the Titans.

Prometheus, Atlas' brother, was a craftsman and one of the cleverest gods. He created man and gave him fire.

Aphrodite was created from the torn-off genitalia of Uranus. She was the goddess of love and beauty, and the Greek counterpart of Ishtar.

Apollo was the son of Zeus (not by Hera) and twin brother of Artemis. He was the god of prophecy, archery, music and medicine. He later became god of the sun.

Artemis, Apollo's twin sister, was the goddess of the hunt. Later, she also became goddess of the moon.

Athena was goddess of war and of the arts. She was said to have sprung fully armed from Zeus' brow. Later on she also became the goddess of wisdom.

Ares was the son of Zeus and Hera. He was the god of war, but where Athena represented glory and honour in war, Ares stood for the evil and brutal aspects of it.

Hephaestus was also a son of Zeus and Hera, and the husband of Aphrodite. He was the god of metalwork and fire. He was born with deformed legs and thrown from Mount Olympus; he landed on the island of Lemnos where he was brought up by the islanders.

Hermes was another of Zeus' illegitimate sons. He was the messenger of the gods and a bringer of good fortune. He was also the god of shepherds and boundaries, and the guardian of graves. It was his job to lead the shades of the dead into the underworld, because he was the only one who could find his way back.

Dionysus was a pre-Hellenic god who was adopted into classical Greek myth as a son of Zeus (but not Hera). He was the god of wine and revelry, with a dangerous side to his nature.

Hecate was a pre-Hellenic moon goddess, and goddess of pathways and crossroads. She was also the patroness of witches. She later became associated with Artemis, and also with the underworld.

Pan is usually, but not always, said to be the son of Hermes and a nymph called Penelope. He was the god of the pastures, who protected sheep and goats. For this reason, he came to be depicted with the horns and legs of a goat.

The myth of creation

There were several stories about how the gods and the world were created. Although there was never one universally accepted version, the account written down by the poet Hesiod in 725 BC gained the widest currency. It is likely that elements of this myth reflect the history of the Greeks and the earlier cultures they had conquered, along with their more primitive gods.

To begin with, there is simply Chaos. Following Chaos – it is unclear whether they are actually his children, but they are usually treated as such – come Gaia (the earth), Tartarus (the underworld), Eros (desire), Erebos (the darkness of the underworld) and Night (the darkness of the earth).

These five beings then create the world. The union of Erebos and Night produces Aither (the bright air of the heavens) and Day (the brightness of the world). And Gaia produces – by herself – Uranus (the sky), the Mountains, and Pontus (the sea).

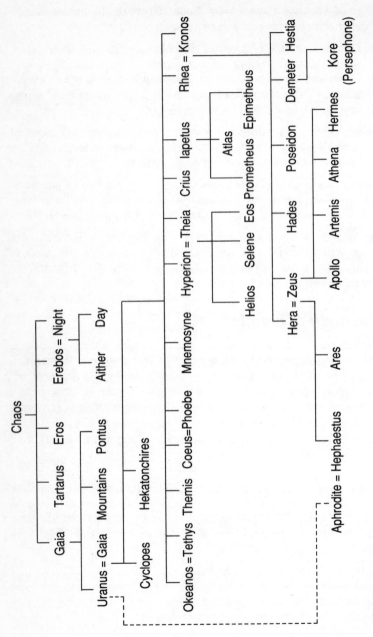

The Greek pantheon

Gaia and her son Uranus then couple to produce the first generation of gods. These fall into three groups:

- three giants with a hundred hands each
- three one-eyed Cyclopes
- twelve Titans; six male and six female.

Uranus is appalled by his children and imprisons them underground, but Gaia incites the youngest Titan, Kronos, to seize power from his father. Kronos does this and, in the process, castrates Uranus. (As with the myth of Osiris, castration symbolises the fact that their reign is at an end, and they are cut down like the corn at harvest time.) Giants, furies and nymphs are created from Uranus' blood, and his genitals fall into the sea and are turned to white foam. From this foam comes Aphrodite, goddess of love and sexual desire.

The Titans then produce the second generation of gods, coupling with each other or with nymphs. Kronos, however, swallows each of his children as soon as they are born because he is afraid that he will be overthrown by one of his children, just as he overthrew his own father.

His wife Rhea, however, tricks him when Zeus is born. She wraps a stone in a cloth and gives it to Kronos to swallow instead of the child. She then hides Zeus in Crete, where he grows up in secret and plans vengeance on his father. He persuades the goddess Metis to serve Kronos an emetic drink which makes Kronos vomit. He regurgitates the stone first, followed by Zeus' five elder brothers and sisters, who help Zeus to defeat the Titans in battle. He is also supported by the Cyclopes and the hundred-handed giants whom Kronos had never released from their prison, but whom Zeus freed.

Zeus is declared supreme ruler of the gods, and decrees that Olympus, the world's highest mountain, will become their home.

The myth of Demeter and Kore

This is a 'food of the dead' myth; it follows the widespread belief that if mortals visit the underworld and eat or drink while they are there, they can never leave. The name Demeter means 'earth-mother', and Demeter was the goddess of the harvest.

The earth goddess Demeter has a daughter by her brother Zeus, whom she calls Kore (which means maiden). Kore is a happy child, and very beautiful. Demeter is worried that Kore may come to some harm since her beauty is so tempting, and takes her to Sicily where she should escape notice.

Unfortunately Hades, god of the underworld, discovers her one day when he happens to be riding past. He decides at once that he wants her to be his wife, and take her down to the underworld where he feels sure she will brighten things up no end. He decides to go and ask his brother Zeus for permission to marry Kore.

Zeus is keen to keep on good terms with his brother Hades, but he knows that their sister Demeter will never agree to let her daughter go. Demeter and Kore both love their freedom too much, and Kore's not the type to be impressed by an honour such as being made queen of the underworld. So Zeus tells Hades that he cannot officially agree to the match, although he will not officially forbid it either. But then he goes on to tell Hades that since he privately thinks it would be a good match for his niece Kore, he will secretly help Hades to kidnap her.

Shortly afterwards, Kore is wandering through the fields of Sicily when she sees a particularly unusual and beautiful flower. She goes over to it for a closer look, not knowing that Zeus has created it to lure her with. As she touches the strange flower, the ground suddenly opens up, and out rushes Hades in a chariot drawn by black horses. He grabs Kore and races back to the underworld with her. Kore keeps screaming for her mother until Hades gets her back to his kingdom, but no one hears her.

Eventually Demeter hears her daughter's screams from a long way off, but when she comes to look for Kore, she finds she has disappeared. No one has seen what happened to her. Demeter lights torches so she can search at night as well as during the day, and she searches for nine days without a rest, but she simply hasn't a clue where Kore has gone.

Demeter becomes so frustrated at not being able to find her daughter that she takes her anger out on Sicily. She withdraws her blessing from the island, causing a drought and making it barren. When this doesn't work, she extends the drought to cover the whole earth. She forbids the seeds to grow and she spoils the crops. Then she has the idea of visiting the sun god, Helios, who sees everything. Helios tells her all about Hades' abduction of Kore, and about Zeus' hand in it.

Demeter is livid with Zeus, and threatens to starve the whole earth so that all the mortals will die and the gods will have no one to rule over or to make offerings to them. Zeus has to relent in the face of this threat, and he tells Demeter that she can have Kore back so long as she hasn't eaten anything while she has been in the underworld. If she has, however, there's nothing he can do since the Fates have determined that no one who eats the food of the dead can return to the world of the living. Zeus sends a message to Hades explaining Demeter's threat and asking him to return Kore to her mother.

Hades tells Kore he is sending her home. But as the chariot is being prepared to take her back, he gives her a pomegranate seed (symbolising marriage) to eat. Kore doesn't know that she isn't supposed to eat the food of the dead, so she takes the seed and swallows it. When Kore, in the chariot, arrives in the field where Zeus has arranged for her to meet her mother, Demeter asks her if she has eaten anything in the underworld. Kore tells her about the pomegranate seed.

Demeter is so upset and angry that she repeats her threat to Zeus. If he can't find a way of letting her have Kore back, she will starve everyone on earth. Zeus can't overrule the Fates, but he manages to come up with a compromise. Kore can spend two-thirds of the year above ground with her mother, from the beginning of spring until after the harvest. But for the remaining four months she must live with Hades as queen of the underworld, where she will be known as Persephone.

Demeter agrees to this arrangement and, every autumn, Persephone returns to her husband in the underworld. Demeter is so lonely she neglects the land and allows it to lie bare. But every spring she and her daughter are reunited, and Demeter brings new growth to the land.

The myth of Prometheus

The name Prometheus means 'forethought'. Prometheus was very clever, and a master craftsman, and he also possessed the power of prophesy. But he was unpopular with the gods for being so kind to mortals; in this myth he gives them fire.

The craftsman Prometheus finds some clay in Boeotia in central Greece, and starts to mould it. He shapes it into figures which have life, and are the first men. But Zeus doesn't like these new creatures, and decides to deprive them of fire and to starve them by demanding so many animal offerings from them that there is nothing left for them to eat.

Prometheus, however, feels sorry for the mortals, and secretly restores fire to them. Then he tricks Zeus by arranging that only the entrails of the sacrificed animals are offered to Zeus, leaving the meat for the humans to eat.

When Zeus realises what Prometheus has done he is furious. In order to punish mankind he creates Pandora – the first woman – and gives her to Epimetheus, Prometheus' brother, despite the fact that Prometheus has warned him to beware any gifts from Zeus. As a wedding gift, Zeus gives Pandora a sealed box which, unbeknownst to her, contains sorrow, illness and other evils: Zeus' way of punishing man.

Zeus learns that Prometheus has tried to warn his brother against marrying Pandora, and his patience finally snaps. He devises the worst punishment he can think of for Prometheus: he chains him to a high rock and, every day, an eagle comes and pecks out his liver. Since Prometheus is immortal his liver restores itself every night, ready to be pecked out again the next day.

Prometheus is released eventually, after thirty years (or a thousand, or even thirty thousand in some versions). Zeus finally agrees to let Prometheus go in exchange for information about the prophecy that one of his sons is destined to be his rival. Heracles is sent to shoot the eagle and to break the chains that are holding Prometheus. Zeus insists, however, that Prometheus wears a ring set with stone from the rock, to remind him of his punishment. This is the first ring to have a setting, and the humans that Prometheus first created wear rings in honour of everything that Prometheus has done for them.

Rome

Most cultures develop their own distinctive mythology, even if it borrows heavily from those of other cultures. So why did the Romans simply take over Greek mythology wholesale, apart from changing a few names? Well, there's a simple answer, and a slightly more complex one.

The simple answer is that Rome was only a single city and, being so small for most of its history, it hadn't developed its own religion by the time it conquered Greece. That is largely true. However, if you go into Roman history in a little more detail, you find that the early citizens of Rome were not an irreligious people. What they had done was to construct a mythology that borrowed almost entirely from its neighbours. The chief of these neighbours were the Etruscans, to the north of Rome, and the Greeks, who occupied the south of what is now Italy, along with a large part of Sicily. The Etruscans had at one time controlled Rome, and they and the Greeks had close trading ties with each other; Etruscan mythology itself was heavily influenced by the Greeks.

This meant that the Romans did have their own gods, but they were already a version of the Greek gods. The main way in which they differed was that the early Romans saw their gods simply as person- ifications of natural forces and, unlike the Greeks, never depicted them in human form. However, as Greek civilisation advanced, their mythology became more sophisticated and complex. The Romans meanwhile continued to worship the more primitive versions of these gods. So when Roman civilisation began to grow and expand its influ- ence, it instantly identified with Greek mythology: it was simply its own mythology taken to a more advanced and highly developed level. It's hardly surprising that the Romans embraced it.

The Romans did have a few myths and legends that were entirely their own, most notably the story of Romulus and Remus (page 59), which is their history of the founding of their city. They also had a number of stories which were consciously fictional, but which they incorporated into their mythology, such as the story of Aeneas. This was written by Virgil in twelve books, the *Aeneid*, in the first century BC, as a tribute to the emperor Augustus. It was modelled on the great Greek epic poems of Homer: the *Iliad* and the *Odyssey*. Homer's epics, by contrast with Virgil's, were written versions of genuine myths.

The Romans also had one significant god who had no Greek equivalent: Janus. He was their original creator god before the Greek influence on their mythology, and he continued to be seen as an important god even after the Romans had absorbed the Greek pantheon, by around 200 BC.

There is another way in which the Romans did more than simply absorb the Greeks' mythology. There are two ways of defining Roman mythology: there is the mythology of the city of Rome itself, and then there is the mythology of the entire empire that was controlled by Rome. So far, we have been looking at the mythology of the city. But the influence of Rome stretched from Britain to North Africa, and from Spain to the Holy Land. They both absorbed and influenced the religions of the peoples they conquered, creating various hybrid mythologies such as the Romano–Celtic myths of north-west Europe. The myth of the Great Mother, Cybele, (page 60) is another good example of this. This process continued across Europe until the Roman empire began to collapse in around 400 AD.

The purpose of the myths

The Romans' early mythology was largely an attempt to explain the world around them. It also included mythologised versions of their own history. But for the last six or seven hundred years of the empire – after the conquest of the Greeks – the Romans adopted a similar attitude to religion to that of the Greeks.

There were differences, however. The Romans were, in a sense, even more civilised than the Greeks. A Greek writer from the first century BC, Dionysius, observed that the Romans had raised the moral tone of the myths. According to Dionysius it was Romulus who had been responsible for this, because when he founded the city of Rome he rejected all the old myths about the gods' bad behaviour.

The Romans were more inclined than the Greeks to use their myths as an example for human behaviour. They favoured the myths that glorified duty and bravery, and they laid great emphasis on the strength and nobility of their heroes. The Romans may have cleaned up the Greek myths somewhat, but in doing so they lost some of their character. The Roman gods never quite achieved the strength of personality that their Greek counterparts had.

One of the best examples of the Romans doing away with the worst excesses of Greek religion is their treatment of the cult of Dionysus. This god of wine and revelry was worshipped in his cult centres by women, known as maenads, who worked themselves into a state of mass hysteria at his festivals. In this condition, they sacrificed goats and occasionally even humans. These practices spread to Italy under the auspices of the Roman god Bacchus, whose followers were called Bacchantes. This cult appalled the Roman authorities, and in 186 BC the Roman senate banned both the cult and the god, after massacring many of its followers.

Religion and politics were combined by the Roman emperors to maximise their control over their people. They deified each emperor, whose image had to take pride of place in all their temples.

The Romans, like the Greeks, had a rational, philosophical outlook on life. As a result, many of the more educated classes were fairly sceptical about many of the religious beliefs of the time. The Roman philosopher Seneca, writing in the first century AD, compared the Etruscans' primitive outlook with the more logical approach of the Romans: 'We hold that lightning is caused by clouds colliding; they hold that clouds collide for the purpose of generating lightning. They attribute everything to the gods, which leads them to believe not that events have a meaning because they happen, but that they happen for the purpose of expressing a meaning.'

The gods and goddesses

With very few exceptions, the Roman gods corresponded to the Greek gods. So the easiest way to understand them, and what their areas of responsibility were, is to relate them to their Greek counterparts.

You'll find, in the list below, that some of the Greek gods are not included. This is because, by the time that Greek mythology had been taken over by the Romans, their importance had waned. In particular the pre-Greek gods, the more animistic ones, tended to retire into the background. As far as the most important gods are concerned, their responsibilities had barely changed since Greek times, apart from the occasional shift of emphasis. For example, Mercury has taken over Hermes' main role as the messenger of the gods, but his secondary interests tend more towards commerce, whereas Hermes was also concerned with boundaries and graves.

Roman deity	Greek equivalent	Function
Janus	(none)	Originally the god of doors and archways, Janus became god of entrances and exits, and then of beginnings and ends. Janus was also the Romans' creator god. He is usually

represented with two faces, one looking each way. In rituals and ceremonies, Janus was always invoked first as the god of beginnings. The opening month of the year, January, is named after him.

Cybele	Rhea	Mother goddess.
Saturn	Kronos	God of seed and sowing.
Jupiter	Zeus	God of the sky and king of the gods.
Juno	Hera	Jupiter's consort.
Neptune	Poseidon	God of the sea.
Dis	Hades	God of the underworld.
Vesta	Hestia	Goddess of the hearth.
Ceres	Demeter	Goddess of the crops.
Proserpina	Kore/ Persephone	Goddess of the underworld.
Venus	Aphrodite	Goddess of love.
Apollo/ Phoebus	Apollo/ Helios	God of medicine, music and poetry. The Romans had no equivalent to Apollo, so they adopted him directly from the Greeks, keeping his name. In his role as sun god he took the name Phoebus.
Diana/ Phoebe	Artemis/ Selene	Goddess of the hunt or, as Phoebe, the moon. (The connection between hunting and the moon is probably derived from the similarity in shape between a hunting bow and a crescent moon.)
Minerva	Athena	Goddess of wisdom and the arts. Also goddess of war.
Mars	Ares	God of war.
Vulcan	Hephaestus	God of fire and the forge.
Mercury	Hermes	The messenger of the gods, and the god of commerce.
Bacchus	Dionysus	God of wine (and much tamer than the Greeks' Dionysus).

The creation myth

The Romans do not appear to have had their own creation myth and, although they would have acquired the Greeks' version of the creation along with everything else they took from the Greeks, they seem to have attached little importance to it.

The only Roman story of the creation is that Janus was the first god, who was there when the elements were still a formless mass. At this stage his name was Chaos. (This is obviously a version of the Greek creation story, although Janus and Chaos are not really equivalent in any other of the myths.) When the elements separated into earth, air, fire and water, Chaos took the form of Janus. The confusion that had reigned until that point was represented by Janus' two faces.

The myth of Romulus and Remus

The name of the city of Rome comes from its mythical founder, Romulus. This story gave the Romans their own identity, and was one of their few entirely original myths. The city of Rome was surrounded by the Sabine tribes, and this story gives a mythical account of the abduction of the Sabine women. Romulus was regarded as a god and identified with the local Sabine god Quirinus, under whose name he was worshipped.

At the beginning of the story, the god Mars seduces a Vestal virgin named Rhea Silva in a sacred grove. As a result, she becomes pregnant, which of course isn't the done thing among Vestal virgins. As a punishment she is imprisoned and, when her twin sons are born, they are abandoned on the banks of the River Tiber to die.

They are rescued, however, by a she-wolf (an animal sacred to the god Mars), who suckles them until they are found by a shepherd, Faustulus, who takes them home and raises them himself. They grow up to be fierce and highly respected warriors, and eventually Faustulus tells them about their birth and early childhood (according to one version, he watched them being abandoned by the Tiber).

Romulus and Remus decide to found their own city in the place where the she-wolf rescued them. But they cannot agree on the exact location. Romulus begins to mark out a boundary ditch around the Palatine hill but Remus makes fun of it by jumping across it. Romulus is so angry that he kills his brother, becoming sole ruler of the new city of Rome. (This is reminiscent of the Hebrew myth of Cain and Abel, of course, of which the Romans would have been well aware.)

Romulus' first problem is how to populate his city. He manages to attract plenty of men by declaring the city a refuge for criminals and runaways from across Italy. But this still leaves him rather short of women. None of the neighbouring women want to marry robbers and thieves. So he devises a plan to resolve the problem.

The local Sabine tribes are on friendly terms (even if their women won't actually go so far as to marry Romulus' band of tearaways) so Romulus invites them to help the people of Rome to celebrate an important religious festival. The Sabine people duly turn up and, at a signal from Romulus, his men abduct all the women and drive their male relatives out of the city.

Not surprisingly, war ensues. Romulus is in luck, however, because Jupiter takes his side and he manages to hold Rome against the Sabines. Eventually, distressed at so much bloodshed, the women themselves intervene and plead with the Romans and the Sabines to make peace. They do so, and the two people agree to unite.

The Sabine ruler, Titus Tatius, rules jointly with Romulus for a short time, until his death. Romulus then rules alone for another thirty-three years. According to one version of the story, Romulus finally disappears suddenly and mysteriously in a thunderstorm.

The myth of Cybele, the Magna Mater

This is an example of a deity who was incorporated into Roman mythology from elsewhere in the empire, as this myth explains. Cybele was an important mother goddess from Phrygia (in north-west Turkey). She was an equivalent of the Greek mother goddesses Rhea and Demeter.

According to the Romans' myth, Cybele used to live on Mount Ida with her consort Attis. But she discovered that he was unfaithful and challenged him. She caused him to go mad and, in remorse, he castrated himself under a pine tree and bled to death. Eventually, Cybele agreed to restore him to life and take him back. The Romans' annual celebrations included ritual blood-letting and self-castration.

It is 204 BC, and the Roman commander Hannibal is fighting the Carthaginians. The Romans want to know the outcome of the war so they consult an oracle, which gives them a strange answer. It tells them that they must seek the mother, and that when they find her, she must be received by someone who is chaste. Confused by this, they decide to double-check with the great oracle at Delphi, in Greece. This oracle, too, tells them that they must fetch the great mother ('Magna Mater' in Latin) who lives on Mount Ida.

The Romans send a message to the king whose territory includes Mount Ida, asking if they can bring the statue of Cybele, the Magna Mater, back to Rome. The king declines their request, but then the goddess herself speaks, saying that she wants to go. The king changes his mind and agrees to let the Romans take her statue back with them.

The statue is loaded on to a specially built boat, and shipped as far as the mouth of the Tiber, where the citizens all come to meet it. But the boat is too heavy to pull ashore, and the Romans are afraid that they will be unable to follow the oracle's advice. Then a woman comes forward – Claudia Quinta – who has been wrongly accused of being unchaste. She prays to the great mother, asking Cybele to allow her to bring the boat ashore if she is innocent. She is, and she brings the boat easily ashore on her own. The statue is safely ensconced in its temple, and Cybele becomes a great goddess in Rome; and her followers hold wild celebrations at her festival every March.

The British Isles

From some time around 500 BC, the British Isles were inhabited by the Celts. The Celtic people occupied huge areas of west and central Europe, and as far east as Asia Minor, by around 200 BC. And yet, compared with other cultures of the same period, we know little about them.

One thing that we do know is that they would never have referred to themselves as Celts. The name was given by the Greeks, who called them Keltoi, to describe the various tribes who occupied these lands to the north and west of them. The Celts themselves, however, would have seen themselves as a number of independent tribes and peoples who shared almost nothing in common; they didn't even speak a shared language – usually one of the most important factors in binding people together.

The most reliable way to learn about ancient societies is through the written material they left behind, but unfortunately the Celts left almost none. They occasionally borrowed other people's alphabets – usually runic – to inscribe headstones or keep basic trading records, but they had no written tradition of their own. So the Celts still puzzle scholars and archaeologists more than many other cultures of the same period or even earlier.

There are two main sources of information about the Celts and their beliefs. Both are helpful, but neither is wholly reliable. Firstly, the Celts may not have written anything down, but many of the people who were contemporary with them did, in particular the Greeks and the Romans. And secondly, many of the Celtic myths survived to be written down centuries later in both Ireland and Wales. Both of these sources need examining in a little more detail.

The Classical writers who visited the Celtic lands certainly brought back genuine accounts of religious ceremonies and beliefs, which must have been largely true. However, these accounts were anecdotal, and Celtic practices would have varied a great deal from tribe to tribe. The reports were somewhat biased as well, since the Greeks and Romans wanted to portray these 'barbarians' as being uncivilised; they found this quite easy since they disapproved thoroughly of many Celtic practices, especially ritual human sacrifice, which they themselves had long since given up.

In order to understand the need for caution in reading the Irish and Welsh myths, you have to know what happened to the Celts. In 54 BC the Romans invaded Britain, although they never really made it across the sea to Ireland. We have already seen what happened to mythologies when the Romans conquered other peoples: they became merged. The Romano–Celtic period (as it is known) began; the gods

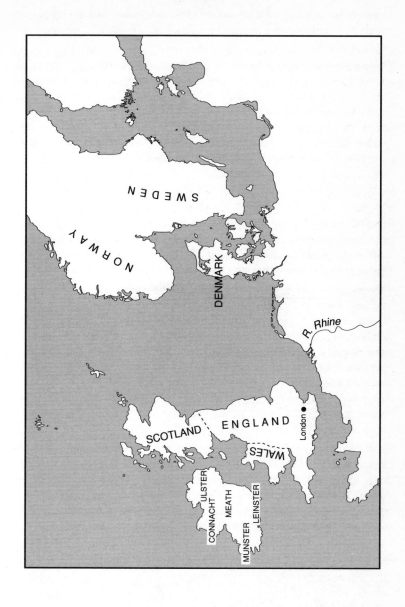

and goddesses became much more widely recognised, instead of being local, and they became identified with Roman deities and took on their attributes.

The Romans left Britain in around 410 AD after about a 130 years of sporadically defending the island against the Saxons. By the time they left, Britain was mainly Christianised. These Britons (the Romanised Celts) were left behind to be overrun by Saxons, Angles and Jutes – pagans from northern Europe. Slowly the Britons were driven further west, into Cornwall and Wales, or were simply absorbed by the invaders. These Christianised Britons, however, managed to bring their new religion to the Anglo-Saxons, backed up by missionaries sent by the Pope. By 460 AD one of the British monks, St Patrick, had also introduced Christianity to Ireland.

The Celtic myths were first written down in the eighth century. Since the time of the Celts, 800 years had passed during which the people of Britain had been Romanised (apart from the Irish) and subsequently Christianised. The myths were then recorded by Christian monks.

This should make it clear that many of the myths would have been lost for ever, and the rest must have been changed hugely. Nevertheless, having no written language of their own, the oral tradition among the Celts was so strong that their stories and myths would have been told from generation to generation by the Britons, long after Celtic culture had officially disappeared from Europe. These myths would have become so changed that the people who told them would most likely have forgotten their origins. But the 'Celtic' stories that were recorded by the monks must have incorporated elements of the earlier stories of the ancient Celts.

However, we are left with only glimpses of the ancient myths, almost all contained within the two great collections of Celtic legends written down by the monks. One of these collections is Irish and the other Welsh. Almost nothing else remains. We don't know, for example, whether the Celts had any kind of creation myth; if they did, it has been lost. The only scant references that remain seem to be so heavily Christianised it's impossible to tell whether anything of the Celts' beliefs remains. We know they had few deities that were recognised other than locally, but we can't even be sure that we have records of the full pantheon. Celtic mythology is frustratingly just beyond our reach, but perhaps this air of mystery is one of the reasons the myths are so popular today.

The purpose of the myths

From what we know, the Celts were a very religious society. Like most primitive cultures, they practised a form of nature religion, and worshipped deities who were the personification of the sky, the mountains, the rivers and so on. Many of their religious ceremonies were an attempt to influence these forces to bring good fortune. These ceremonies often involved animal and even human sacrifices.

The Celts also held some seasonal religious festivals, although the evidence suggests that many of these were celebrated only in certain areas. Samhain, for example, which falls at the beginning of November, was celebrated particularly in Ireland. It is unclear whether the the Celts elsewhere in the British Isles celebrated it, and there is no reference to it at all among the Celts of Gaul (which is now part of France).

In Ireland, Samhain would have been a date for tribal assemblies, law making and other communal activities. It was also the time when livestock would be brought in for the winter (so it may have been a more important festival in areas where stock rearing was more central to the economy). So this would have been an important time to invoke the gods to protect the cattle through the winter. By the time Christianity reached Ireland, Samhain was the most important festival of the year.

The Celts also set great store by bravery in battle, and many of their myths glorified heroes, to set an example to others. It is impossible now to know whether any of these mythological heroes were derived from real people who had once earned a reputation among their fellow Celts for bravery.

Another function of the Celtic mythology was to explain the history of their people. The Irish cycle of myths tells of waves of mythical peoples invading Ireland. Some of these had acquired a heavy Christian overlay by the time they were recorded, but probably bore some relation to the original Celtic myths.

- Cessair comes first, supposedly a granddaughter of Noah, arriving forty days before the flood. All her companions but one are killed in the deluge; Fintan mac Bochra lives for another 5,500 years in the form of a salmon, an eagle and a hawk.
- Parthalon, another descendant of Noah, arrives 300 years after the

flood. He and his people settle the land and begin to farm it. Their enemies are the monstrous Fomorians, who have only one arm and one leg. Eventually, all but one of Parthalon's people are killed by plague.

- Nemedh is the next to arrive. His descendants are almost wiped out, attacking the Fomorians on their island base. The few survivors leave Ireland for the 'northern islands', Britain and Greece.

- Next come the descendants of Nemedh who had gone to Greece. They had been enslaved and forced to create farmland by covering rocks with bagfulls of soil. This is why they are called the Fir Bolg, meaning 'men of bags'. The Fir Bolg divide Ireland between their five chieftains, creating five provinces (Ulster, Leinster, Connacht, Munster and Meath). They institute the first kings, who rule for thirty-seven years.

- The fifth invaders are the Tuatha de Danaan. These people are also descendants of Nemedh – those who fled to the 'northern islands'. They fight the Fir Bolg and then make peace with them, allowing them to stay in Connacht. Then they drive away the Fomorians for good. According to the early Christian histories of Ireland, the Tuatha de Danaan were finally defeated by the Celts and driven underground, where they still live.

By the time the Celtic myths were written down they had acquired a gloss of sophistication that would not have existed in the original versions – the gods had become more humanised, for example – but they still retained a feeling of the importance of nature and natural forces.

The gods and goddesses

When you first study the gods and goddesses of the Celts, they don't seem to fit comfortably with the Celtic myths. There's a good reason for this. Most of what we know about their deities comes from contemporary classical accounts, or from archaeology. These deities had been almost lost by the time their myths were recorded.

Since the Celts were made up of several different tribes, it is hardly surprising that each had its own gods. There were numerous local deities all over the Celtic world, and few that were widely recognised. Some of the more similar local deities became merged over time; it seems that Brighid – who was later Christianised as St Bridget – was quite possibly several local goddesses originally (the name comes from a Celtic word that simply means 'exalted'). These similar local goddesses may have been combined to form one goddess who was more widely worshipped.

The list below concentrates on the Irish and pre-Roman gods and goddesses, since these are the unadulterated Celtic deities, before they became merged with the Roman pantheon. However, it is helpful, at times, to know which Roman deity a particular Celtic deity was merged with as it gives a further clue to their character: they would generally have been combined with gods they already had something in common with.

Irish deities

These are the most important gods and goddesses of the Tuatha de Danaan, the last wave of mythical invaders. Their characters were far more clearly defined than any of the deities who were supposed to have controlled Ireland before them.

Danu was the father of the gods, who were known as the Children of Danu. He was probably a local god of the dead, who evolved into a more widespread god of the underworld. He supposedly lived on an island off south-west Ireland, and instructed the souls of the dead on the route to follow to reach the underworld.

Danu was also sometimes seen as the protector goddess of the Tuatha de Danaan, whose name derived from hers. She may have become a pan-Irish goddess after merging with other mother goddesses, particularly Anu, the tutelary (guardian) goddess of Munster.

The Dagda was the 'good god' and the 'great father'; not father of the other gods, but of the people of Ireland. His symbols were his club, and his cauldron of plenty, which always replenished itself when it had been emptied.

Lugh was known as the many-skilled, and was inventive and clever. The Celtic festival of Lughnasadh (Christianised as Lammas) takes its name from him. He seems to have been recognised further afield than Ireland, and was combined by the Romans with their god Mercury.

Nuada was known as Nuada of the Silver Hand, after his hand was cut off in battle and replaced with a hand modelled in silver. He seems to have been an early chieftain-god.

Macha seems to have been the tutelary goddess of Ulster. She may even have been a Celtic version of a mother goddess worshipped in that part of Ireland even before the Celts arrived. She may have been a fertility goddess but almost nothing is known of her. She seems to have become incorporated into various myths in various roles by authors who knew nothing about her except her name.

Brighid came to be seen as a single goddess, patron of wisdom and divination. According to some sources she had two sisters of the same name, responsible for healing, and for metalwork. This version of the origin of Brighid is the original basis for the modern theory of the Celtic triple goddess. However, there is no contemporary evidence for this view of Celtic mythology.

The Morrigan was a terrifying goddess who attended battles, though she herself never fought, and enjoyed the slaughter.

Welsh characters

These fall into two distinct groups: the Children of Don and the Children of Llyr. These seem to represent two groups of deities who were worshipped successively in Wales. However, by the time the stories were written down, they had become kings and heroes rather than gods. They had clearly changed a good deal; for example, archaeology reveals that local protective goddesses were commonplace in Celtic Britain, and yet no tutelary female characters remain in the Welsh cycle of myths (known collectively as the Mabinogion).

The Welsh myths may have been influenced by those of the Irish, since there was a significant emigration from Ireland to Britain in the late Roman period.

The Children of Don clearly parallel the Tuatha de Danaan, and Don would most likely have been the counterpart of Danu. However, Don is never actually identified, so this cannot be confirmed. The most important of the Children of Don are:

Gwydion: the chief of the Children of Don, he possessed magical powers, and was eloquent and a skilled poet. He seems to have been worshipped chiefly in the north-west of Wales.

Ludd: the counterpart of Nuada, Ludd also had a silver hand.

Llew: the strongest of the gods, and another chieftain-god. He may have been Lugh's counterpart.

Llyr himself doesn't appear in the stories but his name means 'of the sea' so it's likely he started out as a sea god. Incidentally, he was the source for Shakespeare's King Lear, via the twelfth century AD chronicler Geoffrey of Monmouth. These are the most significant of the Children of Llyr:

Manawyddan was the son of Llyr, and seems to be a god of fertility and craftsmanship.

Bran, his brother, was both huge and enormously strong, with supernatural powers. He owned a cauldron which would restore the dead to life if they were placed in it, although they lost the power of speech during the process. He was killed by being wounded in the foot by a poison arrow. (This is reminiscent of the Greek tale of the mighty Achilles, which would have reached Wales via the Romans.) When he knew he was dying he ordered his followers to cut off his head and place it on the White Hill in London facing the continent, to protect Britain against invaders.

There are a few other significant characters in the Welsh mythologies:

Pwyll was a deity who became lord of the underworld after swapping places with its previous ruler for a year and a day.

Rhiannon, Pwyll's wife, was in fact an earlier fertility goddess.

Pryderi, their son, subsequently became lord of the underworld. The four books of the Mabiniogion are about his exploits; he is the only character to appear in them all.

Arthur has a doubtful claim to be Celtic, although he had become incorporated into the Welsh myths by the time they were written down. In fact, he was almost certainly based on a real character, most likely a Romanised Briton who was successful for a time in defending his people against the invading Saxons. This mythologised person may have been amalgamated with an earlier Celtic chieftain-god. Most of the stories about him were not invented until the Middle Ages, and do not figure in the Celtic myths recorded in the eighth century at all. A lot of the history and attributes of the Saxon king Alfred the Great, who ruled at the end of the ninth century, were probably attributed to the Medieval Arthur.

The myth of Finn mac Cumhal and the salmon of knowledge

This is one of the Irish hero myths which is thought to date from about the third century AD. This makes it one of the later stories; perhaps 200 years after the myth of the other great Irish hero, Cu Chulainn. The Irish remained Celtic until they were Christianised in the fifth century – 500 years longer than the rest of Britain – and their myths seem to retain more of the flavour of the early Celts. The British monks, for example, seem to have turned all the Celtic gods into kings and heroes (after all, they themselves believed there was only one god). The Irish monks, by comparison, seem to have allowed the gods to keep their status.

This part of the story of Finn explains how he came by the power of prophecy; divination was important to the Celts, as it is to most cultures that are at the mercy of natural forces. Its popularity can easily be explained if you compare it with a modern-day weather forecast; it may not be 100 per cent reliable, but you still want to know what it says. And the natural forces of the weather and the seasons were of far more importance to the Celts than they are today.

The salmon, incidentally, symbolised divination and prophecy to the Celts because of its uncanny ability to find its way to its spawning grounds.

The story begins with Murna, a granddaughter of Nuada of the Silver Hand. She is married to a warrior chief, Cumhal, who is killed at the battle of Knock. Murna hides in the forest, where she gives birth to a son whom she calls Demna. She is afraid that her husband's enemies will find him and kill him, so she gives him to two old women, to bring him up in the wild woods.

When he is a few years old, Demna goes to find the poet Finn, to learn science and poetry from him. Finn lives on the River Boyne, near a pool in which lives the salmon of knowledge. This fish has acquired supernatural wisdom by eating the nuts that fall from nine hazel trees into the stream below, and it is said that anyone who eats this salmon will enjoy boundless knowledge. The poet Finn has been try-ing for seven years to catch and eat the fish.

Shortly after Demna arrives, Finn succeeds in catching the salmon of knowledge. He gives it to Demna with strict instructions to cook it but to eat none of it himself. When the boy brings the cooked fish, Finn asks him whether he has eaten any of it. Demna says that he hasn't, but that when he turned it on the spit, it was so hot that he burnt his thumb, which he then put in his mouth to ease the pain.

Then Finn the poet tells the boy to eat the fish because, he says, the prophecy about the fish has come true in the boy. He tells the boy that from now on he will be known not as Demna but as Finn, and he sends him away telling him he cannot teach him any more.

Finn (as he is now called) becomes wise and strong, and whenever he needs to know what is happening out of sight, or what will happen in the future, he puts his thumb in his mouth and instantly knows everything he wants to know.

The myth of Culhwch and Olwen

This is one of the Welsh cycle of myths, and the one in which the character of Arthur seems most like a mythical god, whom the monks relating the story have transmuted into a king. It is generally reckoned to be the oldest and most Celtic of the Welsh cycle. The magic cauldron that appears in the story is sometimes thought to be the Celtic forerunner of the Holy Grail which began to appear in later, Medieval tales of Arthur. However, many scholars now believe that the Grail was an entirely Christian invention, with no basis in Celtic myth at all.

Culhwch is the cousin of King Arthur; his mother has died and his father remarried. His new stepmother is jealous of him so she decides to send him off on a long and fruitless quest from which he is unlikely to return. She tells him that he is destined never to marry unless he can win the hand of Olwen. As soon as he hears this, Culhwch falls in love with Olwen, and sets out for King Arthur's court to learn where he can find her.

When he arrives, however, it turns out that Arthur has never heard of Olwen or her family. He promises to look for her, but after a year he returns to Culhwch empty handed. Culhwch is upset and says he will leave, but Arthur, shamed, instructs Kay and Bedivere to accompany Culhwch on his quest. Three other knights join them and the six of them set out.

Eventually they reach a castle, surrounded by a flock of sheep whose shepherd, Custennin, has a dog as big as a horse. Custennin is extremely short tempered, but he likes the look of Culhwch and his party and takes them home with him. It transpires that he is the uncle of Olwen, and his wife is Culhwch's aunt, the sister of his dead mother. She is delighted to see him, but upset to learn about his quest, since he is not the first to seek Olwen as his wife: none of the others has survived.

Custennin explains that his brother, Olwen's father, envies Custennin's share of their father's fortune and has killed all but one of Custennin's sons. So he and his wife are on Culhwch's side in his quest.

The next day Olwen visits the shepherd's house to wash her hair, as she does every week. She is incredibly beautiful and, of course, Culhwch falls even more deeply in love with her now that he has seen her. Wherever she walks, white clover springs from the ground; her name, Olwen, means 'Lady of the White Track'. Luckily for Culhwch, Olwen falls as deeply in love with him, but she explains that he must ask her father's permission to marry her. If she marries without her father's blessing, he will kill her on her wedding day. Under the circumstances, Culhwch decides he'd better get permission for the marriage, so he and his companions call at the castle the next day.

Olwen's father tries to put Culhwch off the marriage with various excuses and, when the party leaves, he throws a poisoned dart after them. Bedivere, however, catches the dart and throws it back, wounding Olwen's father in the knee. He is furious, and curses the companions vigorously. Twice more he throws the dart, and each time Bedivere returns it. At last, Olwen's father agrees to tell Culhwch how to win his daughter's hand.

He must plough, sow and reap a huge hill, all in one day. This can only be done by Amathaon, one of the Children of Don, who won't do it. Likewise, the ploughshare is to be renewed at each headland by Govannon, who won't agree to do it. And Gwylwyld must be persuaded, against all odds, to let his two oxen draw the plough. Next,

Culhwch must find honey nine times sweeter than any made by bees, the magic cauldron which produces any food that is wished for, the sword of Gwrnach the Giant, and dozens more challenges – forty of them in all. Culhwch seems unperturbed, and keeps saying, to every new task, that it is easy and he will achieve it and marry Olwen.

At the end of this list of tasks, the companions set off to complete the challenge. On the way, they happen to meet up with Gwrnach the Giant. Kay pretends to be a sword polisher, and so tricks the giant out of his sword. One down, thirty-nine to go.

When they reach Arthur's court, he promises to help them in the remaining tasks. They all set out again, and the story relates how they complete the remaining thirty-nine tasks, with Arthur's help, by a combination of skill, wiliness and magic. Finally, they manage to obtain the blood of Orddu, the black witch, who lives on the edge of hell. Arthur cuts her in two by throwing his knife at her, and one of the companions catches her blood.

At last they have succeeded, and they set out for the castle of Olwen's father. He concedes defeat, and Custennin's only remaining son cuts off his head. At last Olwen and Culhwch are married, and the group of companions can each return to his home.

Northern Europe

The Norsemen (or Northmen) who settled in Scandinavia had originally been Germanic people who lived east of the river Rhine, in an area that was bordered by the Roman empire. As Rome began to collapse, the Germanic people started to spread out, often invading lands that had previously been under Roman rule. The Germanic Angle and Saxon tribes, for example, settled in Britain.

Other tribes, meanwhile, settled in Scandinavia between the third and sixth centuries AD, and by doing so they escaped the Christianisation that was sweeping the rest of Europe, and retained their own mythology for far longer. By the eighth century the Viking age had begun and it lasted until they, too, were Christianised at the beginning of the eleventh century.

The Vikings were a tough people (they had to be to survive in the harsh Scandinavian climate). Many of their myths feature lands of cold and ice, a motif you don't come across in the mythologies of people from warmer climates. The Vikings were dependent on the sea, since many inland routes were virtually impassable much of the year, and they conducted frequent sea raids on neighbouring countries such as Scotland and Ireland, and both Iceland and Greenland (which they settled). They were driven to find new lands because they didn't have enough farmable land to sustain their own population. They even discovered America 500 years before Columbus, but gave up the attempt to settle it after only three years.

This seafaring tradition is strongly in evidence in the Viking myths, as is their warlike attitude. The myths are full of stories of heroes, battles and violence; a reflection of the people who told the stories, and an example to them. The men who died were all sent to the underworld, Niflheim, apart from those warriors who died in battle. They had the glory of living with Odin in his hall, Valhalla, until the end of the world.

The Vikings were an incredibly cruel and violent race, although less so by the standard of their own times than by modern standards. However, there was a certain fairness about this attitude: they believed that if their enemies treated them in the same way the suffering should be borne bravely, and the victim should forgive his tormentor in the afterlife. The Vikings may seem to be entirely uncivilised, and in some ways they were, when compared with the races around them. But they did have an ethical system, and the myths demonstrate this at times. In the end Ragnarok – the world's end – is brought about because the gods have lied and cheated once too often.

It's worth pointing out that Norse mythology, while essentially Germanic, would have been influenced to some extent by the Romans. To give you one example of this, lynxes were sacred to the moon goddess Freyja, who was the Norse counterpart of the Egyptian Bastet, the Greek Hecate and the Roman Diana. Her chariot was drawn by lynxes, but once the Romans had introduced the domestic cat to Northern Europe – and their goddess Diana – Freyja's chariot began to be drawn by cats instead. If you study the Norse myths, you will find many other references that link in with Greek and Roman mythology.

You will also find that the Viking myths are strongly influenced by Celtic mythology (itself influenced by the Romans) and Christian mythology since most of the lands they raided (such as Ireland) were

Christianised. The Vikings frequently visited Ireland, and even established bases there from which they could raid the rest of Ireland and the British Isles. There is a legend – probably containing more than a grain of truth – that when they settled Iceland, they called in on Ireland en route to collect enough women to populate their new land. This is supposed to account for the character of the Icelanders; they combine the Scandinavian hardiness and fierceness with the Celtic love of poetry and the arts. Certainly the best-surviving early records of the Norse myths are those passed down by the Icelandic poets and written down in the thirteenth century by Christianised Icelandic monks.

The purpose of the myths

The Vikings lived in a strange place, full of glaciers and dreadful weather. They explained much of this as the sound of the frost giants, or Thor throwing his hammer. The Vikings, more than most people, needed to control the elements, and praying to the gods who personified them was the best way for them to do this. The earliest Germanic gods that we know of were just such personifications, but by the time most of the myths were written down they had developed into far more sophisticated characters and stories.

The last ice age in Scandinavia finished around 6000 BC. By this time, early hunters were already living in the region, who settled as farmers around 4000 BC. Some of the Viking myths have elements that are reminiscent of an ice age, especially the land freezing over to signal the beginning of the end of the world. It's possible that this is the echo of a myth picked up from earlier settlers whom the Vikings displaced. The myth of Ragnarok goes on to say that this great freeze will be followed by a great flood; this is precisely what happens when glaciers finally melt.

The gods and goddesses

There were two main families of gods in Norse mythology: the Aesir, who were belligerent sky gods, and the Vanir, who were older, more peaceable fertility gods. The Vanir were presumably older Germanic gods who were largely replaced by the Aesir of the Norse people. There is a myth that the two races of gods fought each other but ended up negotiating a peaceful agreement which included exchanging hostages. The Vanir were the three hostages who went to live with the Aesir.

As with so many mythologies, there were different versions of certain stories at different times or in different places. The relationships between the gods are not always consistent; those listed below are the most commonly accepted. The Viking gods were essentially the same gods who were worshipped by the Anglo-Saxons living in Britain. However, the names were often slightly different; the list below gives Anglo-Saxon names in brackets, where they differ.

The Aesir

Odin (Woden) was the chief god, and Viking counterpart of Zeus and Jupiter. He was the god of the dead, and of those slain nobly in battle; he had an army of warrior spirits, the Valkyries, who brought warriors who died in battle to his hall, Valhalla, ready to defend him when the final battle comes. He was also the god of magic and inspiration. Odin was a harsh and frightening character, and easily roused to anger.

Vili was one of Odin's two brothers; the three of them made the earth, the sky and the sea.

Ve was Odin's other brother. According to some versions of the myths, Ve and Vili once took over Odin's throne (and his wife) when he was away from Asgard on a long journey among the mortals.

Frigga (Frigg), the wife of Odin, and the most important mother goddess, was also the major fertility goddess. Frigga knows everyone's fate, but she will not disclose it.

Thor (Thunor), the second greatest god, after his father Odin, was the strongest of them all. His mother was the earth goddess Fjorgyn. Thor is thought to have derived from the earlier Germanic god of sky and thunder, Donar. Thor was the god of thunder, which he created by throwing his hammer; he generated lightning by striking the hammer against stone. He was a popular god, far more jovial and benevolent than his father Odin (although it wasn't wise to rile him), and he was also responsible for justice.

Sif, Thor's wife, and a corn goddess, was extremely beautiful, with long golden hair, which Loki mischievously cut off while she slept.

When Thor threatened him, he persuaded the dwarves to make Sif a hairpiece out of gold, which became a living part of her as soon as it touched her head.

Balder, the 'good god', son of Odin and Frigga, was loved by all. He is a form of fertility god, but rather than dying and rising again once a year, he will remain dead until the end of the world, when he will rise again.

Hoder was Balder's blind twin brother, who unwittingly killed Balder.

Tyr (Tiw or Tig), god of war, and bravest of all gods, will lose his right arm to the wolf Fenrir at Ragnarok. Tyr is an early god, and the Scandinavian version of the Germanic god Tiwaz. Tiwaz is the Germanic chief god and sky god, and, like Tyr, the god of war.

Bragi, another son of Odin and (usually) Frigga, was the god of music, poetry and oratory. He was sometimes also regarded as the god of wisdom.

Hermod, the messenger of the gods, and the Norse counterpart of the Greek Hermes, was the son of Odin and Frigga, and helped his father by welcoming the fallen heroes of battle to Valhalla (one of Hermes' jobs was to lead the dead into the underworld).

Vidar, another god of war, was known as 'the silent one' because he rarely spoke in the gods' assembly. He is usually thought to be the son of Odin by the giantess Grid. When Odin is killed at Ragnarok by the wolf, Fenrir, Vidar will avenge his death, and survive the end of the world.

Vali was the son of Odin by Rind (goddess of frozen earth). Vali avenged the death of his half-brother Balder by killing another half-brother, Hoder. He will be one of the few gods to survive the end of the world.

Idun, the wife of Bragi, was the goddess of spring and of eternal youth. The Viking gods were not immortal, but they retained their youth by eating the golden apples of eternal youth, guarded by Idun. In one myth Idun is taken prisoner by the frost giants; the gods all start to age, and continue to grow old until she is finally rescued with her basket of apples, and returns them all to youth again.

Loki, the evil god, is generally considered to be the son of two frost giants. He lived in Asgard and was regarded as a god, although his loyalties were always suspect, and at Ragnarok he helps the giants. Loki was extremely clever and cunning and, although sometimes downright evil, he was often portrayed as more of a mischievous or even humorous character.

Hel, daughter of Loki and goddess of the underworld, Niflheim, was thrown into Niflheim by Odin, who decreed that she must rule over men who died of sickness or old age. Hel was cold, but not especially cruel or malevolent, although later Christian writers portrayed her as a monster. She was frightening to look at, however: half her face was human and the other half was blank. The Scandinavian word Hel originally meant simply the place where the dead go, but this became personified into the goddess Hel. The English word, Hell, naturally derives from the Scandinavian.

Heimdall was the guardian of Asgard. He was so alert that he could hear the wool growing on the backs of sheep. Heimdall is an ancient god of light, who was associated with the rainbow bridge that connected Asgard with Midgard. He was also a god of beginnings, and corresponds to the Roman Janus.

Hoenir, associated with divination, and with giving senses and emotions to humans, was given as a hostage to the Vanir when the Aesir and the Vanir made peace.

Ull was the son of Thor's wife, Sif, and therefore Thor's stepson. He was the god of winter, hunting, death and skiing. He was an important god in early Viking mythology, but was later eclipsed by younger gods. In some versions of the myths, he is obliged to spend the summer months with Hel, so that Odin can take charge of the weather.

The Vanir

Njord was a fertility god, the god of sea and winds, and father of Frey and Freya. His wife (and their mother) is Skadi, the daughter of a giant, but he prefers to live by the coast while she chooses to live in the mountains. He and his children are hostages to the Aesir and live in Asgard.

Frey, was god of peace, prosperity, fertility and sex. His symbol was a golden boar, or a giant phallus. He had a magic ship which he could fold up and put into a pouch when he wasn't using it.

Freya was the counterpart of her twin brother Frey, she was also the goddess of love, and known for being free with her sexual favours. Her chariot was drawn by cats and she was symbolised by a golden pig. She also wore a magical necklace, the Brisingamen. According to many versions of the myths, at the end of a battle Freya chose half the men who had died to live with her. The remainder then joined Odin in Valhalla. All women and children who died joined Freya, who was therefore also a goddess of death.

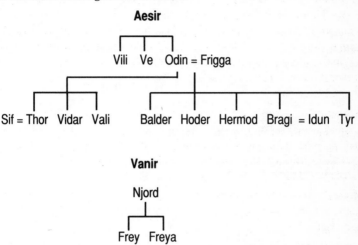

The Viking pantheon

Viking mythology included not only the gods but also numerous giants, some of whom gave birth to gods, in much the same way that the Greek Titans did. These giants were simply personifications of natural forces such as hurricanes, volcanoes and earthquakes; consequently they were figures of fear. According to the creation myth, they were created before the gods, so it seems probable that they were in fact earlier, animistic deities that the Vikings took over and incorporated into their view of things.

The creation myth

In the beginning, there is a great abyss bordered by ice on one side and fire on the other. The ice and fire blend to create the primeval god Ymir, who creates the giants (by means of his legs copulating with each other while he is asleep), and the first man and woman (from the sweat of his left armpit). Ymir has a cow, which licks the salty blocks of ice until three creator gods appear, Odin, Vili and Ve, who promptly kill Ymir. They use his body to form Midgard (the earth), his blood to create the sea, and his skull to form the sky. Maggots are crawling in his flesh: they turn these into either dwarves or fairies, and they set four of the dwarves to hold up the four corners of the sky.

Now there is a circle of earth surrounded by the sea. The world serpent lives in the depths of the ocean and the world tree, Yggdrasil, grows from the centre of the earth.

A hart is eating the levels of the tree, with huge rivers flowing from its horns. There is a goat, too, which yields mead rather than milk, for the warriors of Valhalla to drink. The fruits of this tree will help to ease the pain of childbirth, and the tree is constantly refreshed by having holy water sprinkled over it by the three Norns, the goddesses of destiny (Being, Fate and Necessity – clearly closely related to the three Fates of Greek mythology). The holy water that dripped from the bottom branches became honey.

All the worlds are positioned up and down the tree's trunk and roots. Midgard is the world of the mortals. The fairies and light elves live above this in Alfheim, and above this is Asgard, the realm of the gods. At the top of the tree is an eagle, who sees all of heaven, earth and the underworld and reports to the gods. According to some versions, Asgard is among the roots of the tree; either way, it is more commonly accepted that the Vanir live beneath the earth, in Vanaheim. Jotunheim, land of the giants, is beneath the tree, and so is the land of the dead, Niflheim, which is separated from Asgard by a river with a bridge over it.

Beneath Niflheim is Hvergelmir, a cauldron that feeds twelve rivers with water. And in the cauldron is a great dragon, Nidhug, who gnaws constantly at the roots of the tree. When he kills the tree, the world will end. A squirrel named Ratatosk runs constantly up and down the tree, carrying messages between the eagle and Nidhug.

The Vikings also believed that the world would end, at Ragnarok (meaning 'the twilight of the gods'). This will start with the Fimbul-winter, when the world freezes for three years, and dissent, battles and fratricide break out. The giants, gods and monsters will destroy each other in battle, and eventually the whole world will be consumed in ice and fire, to be born again in a new, fresh form, with gods who were not a party to the mistakes and bad behaviour of the Aesir and Vanir that led to Ragnarok.

The theft of Thor's hammer

The first written record of this myth dates from around 900 AD. It is a good example of the humour that was a frequent element in Norse myth, and it also demonstrates the side of Loki that was not so much evil as clever and fond of mischief.

This myth begins with Thor's discovery that he has lost his hammer. This is particularly terrible because it is the only weapon he has which is effective against the frost giants. What is more, it turns out that the frost giants themselves have stolen it. Their king, Thrymr, then announces that he won't return the hammer unless Thor gives him the goddess Freya in marriage. But Loki persuades Thor that he can recover his hammer if he disguises himself as Freya and goes in her place, with Loki accompanying him disguised as a maidservant. Loki points out that this will not only get Thor his hammer back, but it will also be a great joke.

So the two gods, dressed as women, arrive with Thrymr for the wedding. But Thor nearly gives the game away entirely when he astounds Thrymr by eating a whole ox, eight salmon, and countless delicacies. He washes this down with three barrels of beer. It is only Loki's quick thinking that saves them. He explains that Freya has not eaten for eight days because she is so overexcited about the wedding.

Thrymr accepts this, and is overcome with love for Freya. He lifts her veil to kiss her, but when he sees her face he leaps backwards. He is astounded at how fiery her eyes are. The clever Loki, however, tells him that Freya has not slept for eight days either.

This explanation satisfies Thrymr, who responds by producing the hammer which he agreed to exchange for Freya. He lays it on her lap as a blessing and Thor grasps it, kills the bridegroom and all the wedding guests, and returns triumphantly with Loki to Asgard.

The death of Balder

Balder is a fertility god, and the story of his death, descent to the underworld and eventual rebirth signifies this. In Norse mythology, however, this cycle is presented as lasting for an age rather than taking only a year. In this story, mistletoe plays an important part. To the Norse people, mistletoe symbolised regeneration and rebirth (as it did for the Celts) because it seems to grow magically with no roots in the ground, and also because it is evergreen.

Balder the good is the favoured second son of Odin. He dreams that his life is in danger, and consults the other gods as to what he should do about it. They decide that he should receive immunity from all danger so Frigga, his mother, exacts promises from all things – the elements, metals, plants, trees, animals, poisons, diseases and so on – that they will not harm Balder.

After this, one of the gods' favourite games is to get Balder to stand up when they are all assembled, and throw things at him, hit him, shoot arrows at him and generally amuse themselves watching him survive all their attacks.

The evil Loki, however, is not amused. He dresses up as a woman and visits Frigga. He draws her into conversation about the oath that all things swore not to harm Balder, and asks her if there was anything at all that did not swear the oath. Frigga replies that there is a shoot growing on a tree to the west of Valhalla, called mistletoe. It seemed so young that it couldn't possibly harm anyone, so she thought there was no need to ask it to swear.

Loki goes straight to the mistletoe and picks it; he peels off the leaves and sharpens the twig into a sharp point. Then he returns to the assembly, where the gods are still throwing things at Balder. He sees Balder's blind brother, Hoder, and asks him why he isn't throwing anything at his brother. Hoder explains that he has nothing to throw and, anyway, he can't see to aim.

Loki offers Hoder the stick he is carrying, and tells him that he will direct him where to aim. Hoder follows his instructions and the mistletoe twig goes straight through Balder's heart and kills him. The gods are speechless at the sight of their friend lying dead. At last

Frigga asks the gods whether any of them is brave enough to ride to Hel, goddess of the underworld, and offer her a ransom if she will return Balder.

Balder's brother Hermod agrees to go and, while the other gods take Balder's body to the sea to be cast loose on a burning boat, Hermod rides for nine nights through dark valleys until he reaches the gates of Hel's kingdom. He tells Hel how upset the gods are and asks her to return Balder to them. Hel says, however, that she isn't convinced that Balder is as well loved as Hermod claims. So she makes a condition: she will release Balder only if all things in the world, alive and dead, weep for him.

Hermod returns to Asgard and tells the gods about Hel's condition. They send messengers out across the world, asking all things to help weep Balder out of Hel's kingdom. Everything in the world agrees to weep for Balder, except for one giantess. She refuses, saying that Balder means nothing to her and she doesn't care if he stays with Hel for ever. She cannot be persuaded to cry, and eventually the messengers have no choice but to give up and return to Asgard, and break the bad news to the gods.

The gods are not only deeply upset but also very angry, because they realise that the giantess was Loki in disguise. They set out from Asgard to take revenge on him, but Loki has already fled, guessing that they would see through his disguise. Eventually the gods close in on Loki, and he turns himself into a salmon to escape them. But Thor is too clever, and manages to capture him.

In punishment, the gods take Loki to a dark cave. They capture his two sons and turn one of them, Fenrir, into a wolf, who then eats his brother. They drill a hole in each of three rocks and tie Loki to them using his dead son's intestines, which have become as hard as iron. Finally, they hang a snake above his head, which constantly drips searing poison on to his face. At last they go back to Asgard, leaving Loki imprisoned until the end of the world.

Fenrir finds his mother and leads her to Loki, but there is little she can do. In an attempt to make his life more tolerable, she holds a bowl under the snake to catch the venom and keep it off Loki's face. But the bowl fills up and every time she removes it momentarily to empty it, the poison once again runs down Loki's face and burns his skin.

As for Balder, he is trapped in the underworld until the end of the world, Ragnarok, arrives. Then the gods and the giants kill each other, and the earth crumbles. Eventually it is covered by a great flood. Finally, when everything has gone quiet, a new earth rises from the sea, fresh and fertile. Balder leaves the kingdom of Hel to join the young gods who have survived and to help them build a new and better world.

4
FAR EASTERN MYTHOLOGY

India

The historical links between Indian culture and the cultures of Europe and the Middle East are stronger than you might imagine. To understand why, you have to go back to the invention of the wheeled vehicle.

In the third millenium BC, the Aryan nomadic cattle and sheep farmers of the steppe lands north of the Black Sea started to domesticate some of the local wild animals: the horse and the camel in particular. These nomads, closely related to some branches of the more settled peoples of Asia Minor, needed to travel far afield to find new grazing lands for their cattle and sheep in the hostile steppe lands. The horse, in particular, made this possible: they had always had to travel along the more accessible watercourses before, but the horse could travel across far rougher terrain, carrying people on its back, and enabling them to search out new pastures far more easily.

Soon, wheeled carts were invented in the Caucasus, and their use soon spread among the other Aryan tribes of the steppes. This meant that these nomadic farmers could travel further than ever before, carrying their families and luggage on horse-drawn carts, and their economy became far more successful. They began to spread to the west and the east; and some of them travelled beyond the Caspian Sea and down the east side of it and arrived, eventually, in the fertile Indus valley in the north-west of India. This was the birthplace of Indian civilisation; an earlier (unrelated) people, the Dravidians, had built the first Indian cities on the banks of the Indus.

The Indo-European invaders weren't slow to occupy this new territory and push the Dravidians further south. The Indus valley offered the Aryans a fertile region – on a par with the river basins of the Nile and the Tigris–Euphrates – where they could settle and build their own first cities.

These early Aryan settlers built a culture that survived for a thousand years, from 2550 BC. They were finally displaced, half way through the second millenium BC, by a further invasion of Aryans who had taken the same route through the steppes but who had stopped for a time in what is now northern Iran, and finally reached the Indus valley in 1550 BC.

These Aryans and their predecessors spoke a language that was in the same group – Indo-European – as the language of parts of Asia Minor where they had come from. And their history only began to separate from that of Asia Minor between 2500 and 1500 BC, long after the Mesopotamian and Egyptian cultures had begun to flourish. What's more, there were strong trading ties between the two areas, along trade routes that ran from Europe across Mesopotamia and Persia into north-west India. So the similarities that exist between European, Middle Eastern and Indian mythologies are not so strange as they might at first appear.

The earliest recorded mythology of the area is that of the Aryan people, whose beliefs were recorded in the Vedas, a cycle of mythic hymns and rituals dedicated to their gods. The Aryans passed down the Vedas only by oral tradition for hundreds of years, but eventually they were recorded in their language, Sanskrit, which is closely related to Greek and Latin.

The Aryans eventually settled most of northern India by around 500 BC. Although they began as nomadic hunters and farmers, they quickly adopted the more settled way of life of the Indus valley. They were already attributing a sacred status to their precious cattle; one of their myths tells how their hero-god, Indra, gave cows to the people by liberating the gods' cattle from a cave. They were also starting to attach great importance to social caste; an attitude that still influences modern Indian society.

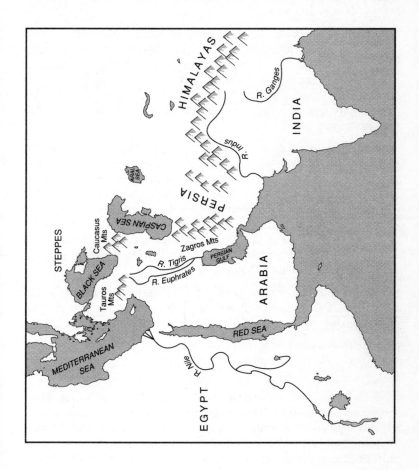

This culture gradually spread to cover the whole of India, and the people became known as Hindus (meaning 'of the Indus'). The Hindu religion evolved out of the Aryan, or Vedic, religion and – as so often happens – the earlier gods were relegated to minor roles and later Hindu gods took prominence. This shift happened slowly, between about 900 and 500 BC.

Hinduism has arguably the most complex and comprehensive mythology in the world. India is still a country of numerous tribes and languages. Hinduism has developed over thousands of years and has incorporated elements of all these cultures to produce a mythology that is both sophisticated and full of contradictions. It contains cults that believe in rich, lavish festivals, and others that follow the path of asceticism and meditation.

One of the most important developments of Hinduism was the concept of reincarnation: after death, we will be reborn to live another life. This concept is followed through in their image of the world, which is created, flourishes, decays and dies, only to be recreated in an unending cycle. Even their great god, Vishnu, has three stages: Brahma, the creator; Vishnu, who preserves life on earth; and Shiva, the destroyer. Shiva is followed by Brahma, who creates the world again. This idea of reincarnation and the cycles of nature is a constant theme in Hindu mythology.

The Hindus also developed the idea of karma, which states that each life is affected by how well or badly we have behaved in previous lives, and how we lead this life will affect the next life.

The early Vedic and Hindu writings fall broadly into three categories.

- **The Vedas**: these date from around 2000 BC but were not actually written down until much later. They were recorded in four collections: the Rig-Veda, the Yajur-Veda, the Sama-Veda and the Atharva-Veda. During the later (Brahmanic) phase, each of these was supplemented with a further sacred treatise; these are known collectively as the Brahmanas.
- **The Epics**: the two great, early Hindu epic poems were written between about 400 BC and 400 AD. These were the Ramayana (dating from around 300 BC) and the Mahabharata. The famous Bhagavad-Gita, composed in about 200 BC, is part of the Mahabharata. Around this time the Upanishads, early Hindu sacred texts, were also written.

- **The Puranas**: later Hindu accounts of the myths of their gods, and the creation, destruction and recreation of the universe. The Puranas became the most important Hindu sacred texts from about 400 AD onwards.

The purpose of the myths

The Vedic gods, or Devas, were animistic: personifications of storms, fire, ritual and so on. The later Hindu gods represented the new Hindu culture taking over from the earlier Aryan people. Since this was a gradual assimilation rather than a conquest, the gods were assimilated into the mythology rather than deposed. They retained the deep respect of the Hindu people, even though many of their roles became less significant.

Many of the Hindu myths tell of events in their history, some of which pose a continuing threat to their culture. There are myths about both drought and flood, two of the greatest fears for the people of India.

Another function of the myths was to perpetuate the caste system. The Aryan invaders would have settled in family clans, since these were crucial to the nomadic way of life they had been leading until then. Each clan would be descended from a common male ancestor. These clans were the forerunner of the caste system, and the Vedic and Hindu religions were designed to reinforce this. The Hindu concept of *dharma* is an integral part of their social structure; a pattern of behaviour that is appropriate to a person's social position.

The Aryan people had three levels of society: the warrior nobility, the priests (Brahmans), and the ordinary people. Each of these practised essentially the same religion, but each with their own rites. As this system developed into the more complex caste system, it moved from the Vedic stage to what is known as the Brahmanic stage. Vedic and, especially, Hindu mythologies frequently emphasise the importance of order and the need to maintain it.

Gods and goddesses

As with most mythologies of such complexity, there are numerous gods, and numerous versions of many of the stories. This is a list of the most important deities, and the most common versions of the myths about them.

The early Vedic gods were often incorporated into later Hindu mythology, but they sometimes changed function and usually reduced in importance.

Dyaus The first creator-god, the name Dyaus is related to the Greek Zeus, the Latin word *deus*, meaning 'god', and the Germanic Tyr. According to Vedic tradition Dyaus and his consort Prthivi created the rest of the Vedic pantheon between them, and ordered heaven and earth.

Indra The king of the gods as well as being a weather god, associated with rain and fertility, who displaced Dyaus, perhaps because the Aryan people wanted a god who was more use in the dry, hot climate of their new land. Indra was a hero-god, and far more humanised than the other deities. Like Prometheus in Greek myth, he had a special interest in the welfare of humans. Indra remained as nominal head of the later Hindu pantheon, but he lost his power to Vishnu.

Maha Devi An early mother goddess, and vegetation goddess, whose worship survived into Hindu mythology. She became a composite goddess who embodied all the Hindu goddesses. In a related form she is also Devi, the most important deity in the Hindu pantheon.

Agni The god of fire, Agni's importance was drastically reduced in later mythology, although when he is in a destructive mood he is often seen as an aspect of Shiva. He has seven arms and often has the head of a goat.

Soma The god of water, and the personification of the sacred drink soma, he was sometimes presented as the god of ritual. He later became the moon, believed to be made of soma, whose waxing and waning was thought to be caused by the gods removing the soma each month to drink, and give themselves strength.

Savitar The driving force, Savitar is a form of sun god who causes the sun, the winds and the water to move. He is golden, and kindly, and gives immortality to the other gods. He has the power to forgive sins, and he leads good souls to heaven.

Mitra The god of intimate friendship, Mitra was also a sun god. The sun was of great importance, and various gods represented different aspects of it. Mitra is the same god as the Persian Mithra (who originated in what is now Iran). Mithra was a god of light, who was associated with the god Ahura Mazda. The Romans adopted him, and he became the centre of a popular cult under the name Mithras.

Varuna The brother of Mitra, Varuna was associated with the moon. Since the moon is the land of the dead, he is also known as the king of the dead. He is responsible for regulating the movement of water, and bringing rain. He is thought to correspond to the Persian god Ahura Mazda.

Surya Another sun god, Surya is the sun, riding across the sky in a golden chariot. He is often described as being too intense, as the sun often is in India. When he married, his wife left him because she could not stand the fierceness of his attention.

Yama The Vedic god of the dead, who became the Hindu god of death. He is the twin of Yami, goddess of death, and came to be represented as a punisher of humans who was green in appearance.

The Hindu pantheon is dominated by three gods: Brahma, Vishnu and Shiva. As often happens in Hindu mythology, these three are all versions of the same god (rather like the Christian father, son and holy spirit trinity). In their separated forms, they also have other names for other aspects of themselves. In a sense, Hinduism is monotheistic since all the gods are aspects of one supreme force.

Brahma The first god, Brahma was created from a surge of consciousness. He is a benevolent creator-god and god of knowledge, and also the guardian of the Vedas. He will live for a hundred years, and he is still only fifty-one, since each day and night, or *kalpa*, of his life lasts for 8,640,000 earthly years. At the end of each of his years, the universe is destroyed and recreated. He has four heads, one facing in each direction. When his wife was born (or, in some versions, his daughter) she was so beautiful that he grew a head facing each way so that he could see her whichever side of him she was.

Saraswati The goddess of wisdom and wife of Brahma. She probably started out as a Vedic river goddess, but she is now a mother goddess, fertility goddess and patron of the arts. Saraswati is essentially another aspect of Brahma; his *Shakti*. This is his feminine or creative power. This notion of Shaktis was developed in later Hindu times, and every male deity has one.

Vishnu The benevolent preserver of life, Vishnu was originally another Vedic god who rose to become the most powerful god of all, eclipsing Indra. His name means 'far-strider' because when the cosmos was ordered he measured it out with three huge strides. Vishnu rules human time, and keeps a moral balance through the concept of karma. When the world is in great danger, he incarnates himself in human form (known as an avatar) in order to defend it. He will do this ten times; so far he has incarnated nine times; the ninth avatar was the Buddha, created to lead the sinful into temptation to ensure their punishment.

Laksmi The goddess of fortune and wife, or Shakti, of Vishnu. Laksmi represents the ideal Hindu wife, subservient and loyal. She is incarnated alongside each of Vishnu's avatars.

Rama Vishnu's seventh avatar, whose heroic exploits are at the core of the *Ramayana*, one of the most important Hindu epic poems, written in Sanskrit in around 300 BC. Like Homer's *Iliad*, it is the story of a hero who sets out to regain his wife who has been abducted. These two stories are so similar in outline that it is thought that they both date back to a common source, some time before 1000 BC.

Krishna The eighth avatar of Vishnu, he appears in the epic the *Mahabharata*. Krishna symbolises human hopes and failings; he is a hero-god, but he is also prone to overindulge in wine, women and song. His chief role as an avatar was to rid the world of the evil king Kansa. According to the Mahabharata he started life as a cowherd, and it is likely that he was originally a fertility god associated with herdsmen.

Shiva The destroyer, evolved from a Vedic storm god called Rudra; he is sometimes known as Shiva-Rudra. Rudra himself may have developed from an even earlier, pre-Indo-European god. Shiva's neck is blue because he holds in his throat the primal poison which he eventually swallows to save mankind from it. Shiva is an ascetic, who spends most of his time in the mountains. Shiva's symbol is the lingam, or phallus, often accompanied by the yoni, the vulva.

Shakti The feminine aspect of Shiva, who especially appears in her violent aspects as Durga or Kali (see below).

Devi The principal female goddess, the word devi also means a female deity. She is a development of the Vedic Maha Devi, or mother goddess. In some versions she is the consort or Shakti or Shiva. She appeared as Durga to destroy the buffalo monster that none of the other gods had the courage to face, and as a result became the greatest of the Hindi deities. Devi has many forms, some of which are gentle and benevolent and some of which are terrifying.

Durga   The warrior goddess was created by the gods to kill the buffalo monster; she has either eight or ten arms and rides on the back of a tiger. She later became the goddess of the Thugs, a caste of hereditary murderers.

Kali   The goddess of destruction, and an aspect of Devi. Kali, known as 'the dark one', has fangs and wears a necklace of human heads; she has at least ten arms, and sometimes as many as eighteen. Her role is to destroy the demons who threaten the order of things, but she becomes so drunk on killing that she is in danger of destroying the world. She kills her own husband, Shiva, and dances on his body before she realises what she is doing and comes to her senses. She occasionally appears in a more benign aspect, since the Hindus believe that from destruction comes creation. Kali is related to the Egyptian Hathor and the Celtic Morrigan, among others.

Parvati   The youngest of Devi's benign aspects, and a goddess of fertility. She personifies the perfect wife as one of the aspects of Shiva's consort; she was originally dark skinned but Shiva goaded her about it so much that she went to great lengths to become golden skinned. In some versions of the myths it is her discarded dark skin that becomes Kali.

Skanda   The god of war, and son of Shiva and Parvati. He was created when the gods persuaded his parents to put a stop to their constant sexual activity. This resulted in a huge amount of unused semen, which Brahma put on the mountain of the rising sun. After 10,000 years, it turned into Skanda.

Ganesha   The god of wisdom, who clears the way to success, Ganesha has the body of a man and the head of an elephant (it is his trunk that clears obstacles on the path to success). He is the son of Shiva and Parvati. After her unconventional attempt at motherhood which resulted in Skanda, Parvati wanted her own child who would guard her. She created Ganesha, according to some versions, from the skin she rubs from her body when she is bathing. She then set him to guard her outside the room. Shiva attempts to enter and Ganesha forbids him so Shiva, known for his short temper, knocks Ganesha's head off. Parvati insists that Shiva restore him to life so Shiva grabs the first head he can find, which is an elephant head. Ganesha is gentle and benign, and a popular god among the Hindu people.

Hanuman   The clever monkey god, who accompanies the seventh avatar of Vishnu – Rama – on his exploits. Hanuman symbolises the faithful servant. He moves incredibly fast (his father is the god of winds), can change into any shape, and leads an army of monkeys. He is a popular character in Hindu mythology, and is worshipped especially in villages.

The myth of creation

As you would expect with a complex mythology that is largely created by assimilating other mythologies, there is more than one creation myth. Many of them include the hiranyagarbha, or golden egg, from which the world is hatched. This version is from one of the Brahmanas, the sacred texts that were added to each of the Vedas.

The primordial waters produce a golden egg, which contains all the lands, seas and mountains, the sun and the planets, the humans, gods and demons, and all the other raw ingredients from which to construct a universe. After a thousand years, the egg gives birth to Brahma, the creator.

Brahma sets about meditating and creating the universe, but he sees that the earth is submerged beneath the oceans. He takes the shape of a wild boar, dives down, and raises the earth up with his tusks, to sit above the oceans. He then completes the task of assembling the universe into a more ordered form.

The myth of Indra and the dragon

Indra was originally a heroic leader in the Aryan conquest of India, but he was later made a god. Before the Brahmans and Hindus made Vishnu the chief god, the position was held by Indra. He was associated with rain and fertility, and he wielded a thunderbolt which he used to kill the drought demons. Indra's heroic exploits are recorded in the Rig-Veda, first of the Vedas; this is the version told here. Later, in the Hindu Mahabharata, which was written between 300 BC and 300 AD, Indra's importance waned and, as a reflection of this, he was defeated by the dragon at the end of the story.

> The fortifying soma, which Indra drinks to give him strength, was a hallucinogen which was widely used by Vedic priests and plays an important part in the Vedas. The priests used to sacrifice soma to the gods, and believed that without it the gods would not have the strength to govern the world.

The evil dragon Vritra swallows the earth's seven rivers and imprisons them in his mountain. Then he lies down on the mountain top and guards them against anyone who might come to steal them.

Gradually, without the rivers, the land becomes parched, and the grass and plants begin to die. Even the trees are struggling for survival. The people pray to the gods to help them, but none of the gods is strong enough to challenge Vritra. They buy all the food they can; then they beg all the food they can. In the end, even the rich have no food left, and slowly the people begin to starve. They beg the gods to come and help them before they all die.

The gods don't want to see their people die, but they know there is nothing they can do against Vritra. But Indra, the youngest god, is determined to help the people if he can. He prepares three bowls of soma, and drains them one by one. He feels his strength growing with each bowlful, and by the time he has drunk all the soma he knows he has become the strongest of the gods. He takes his thunderbolt and sets out to fight the dragon.

Vritra is sitting on top of his mountain, and he sees Indra coming. He opens his huge mouth and breathes out a blackening fog. Then he breathes blinding lightning, deafening thunder and razor-sharp hailstones. To his surprise, Indra is not afraid. Despite the lightning and thunder he is not blinded or deafened, and the hailstones haven't cut him. He takes advantage of the next lightning bolt to take aim and hurl his thunderbolt at the dragon. It kills Vritra, who falls to the foot of the mountain far below. At this, Vritra's mother emerges from the mountain to avenge her son, but Indra is not afraid, and kills her too with his thunderbolt.

Finally, Indra uses his weapon to break open the mountain and release the seven rivers. They rush down the mountain and across the land, filling the dry river-beds. The grass, crops and trees begin to revive and the people are saved by their great god Indra.

The myth of the churning of the ocean

This is the story of how the gods achieved immortalilty: it is also a classic good versus evil myth. It tells of the conflict between the Devas, or gods, and the Asuras, or anti-gods, shortly after the creation. It also explains the waxing and waning of the moon. This myth is first found in the Vedas, but remained popular: this version is taken from the Hindu *Mahabharata*.

The gods are gathered on Mount Meru, discussing how they can come by the elixir of eternal life, when Vishnu has an idea. He suggests that they throw strong herbs into the sea, and precious jewels, and then churn the sea in order to produce the elixir.

They need a paddle to stand in the ocean and rotate to create the churning motion. So they uproot Mount Mandara and balance it on the back of a submerged tortoise. In order to rotate it, they take the snake Vasuki and wrap him around the paddle, with a length of his tail protruding at one end, and his head and neck at the other. Pulling alternately from each end, they should be able to make the paddle turn back and forth.

However, it takes all the Devas to pull at one end, so they have to ask the Asuras to come and pull the other end for them in exchange for a share in the elixir. The Asuras agree, and a sort of co-operative tug-of-war ensues, with the Devas pulling one end, the Asuras pulling the other, and the paddle spinning back and forwards in the middle. The friction is so great that the trees on the mountain catch fire, but Indra quenches the fire with his rain.

Eventually, their churning produces the sun, the moon, several gods and goddesses, and other treasures and, at last, the divine physician holding the elixir of eternal life. The evil Asuras snatch the elixir before the Devas can reach it, but Vishnu takes the form of a beautiful woman and distracts their attention so the Devas can recover the precious elixir.

However, one of the Asuras, Rahu, manages to snatch a drop of it. But as he is about to swallow it, Vishnu beheads him. Having taken a sip of the elixir Rahu cannot die, but Vishnu takes his head and places it in the heavens, where it chases the sun and the moon for ever. The elixir, or soma, is identified with the moon, and the waning and waxing of the moon is explained by the elixir disappearing down Rahu's throat and then reappearing. When Rahu catches up with the sun he swallows it, causing an eclipse.

In case you were wondering, when the gods have finished churning the ocean they take Mount Mandara and put it back where they got it from.

China

China has been continuously inhabited since at least the time of 'Peking Man', around 500,000 BC, and *homo sapiens* developed in around 300,000 BC. When it comes to the start of the first civilisations, however, China was almost entirely isolated from the rest of the world by the mountains and steppes to the north, south and west, and by the sea to the east.

Despite this, the start of Chinese civilisation dates to much the same period as the civilisations of the Mediterranean and India. The Shang dynasty began in around 1500 BC, probably as a collection of village clans, but with a king based in a capital city. And like the other great early civilisations of Mesopotamia, Egypt and India, the Shang also built their new civilisation in the fertile valley of a great river, the Yellow River.

In fact, China can't have been quite so cut off as it is often credited with being; there would have been some trade with nomads and wandering merchants along the borders. This is evident for a number of reasons. For example, the Chinese were spinning silk from at least 1200 BC, but the silk moth wasn't native to China. It came from India. The Chinese, though, seem to have been the first to work out how to spin a continuous thread from its cocoon. The first form of money in China was the cowrie shell, which was not indigenous to its shores; they probably came from the Maldive Islands the other side of India. The wheat that they grew, too, must have originated in the west.

There is another interesting link between early China and the West. At about the same time that the Shang civilisation was starting up in the Yellow River valley, some of the Indo-European peoples who had

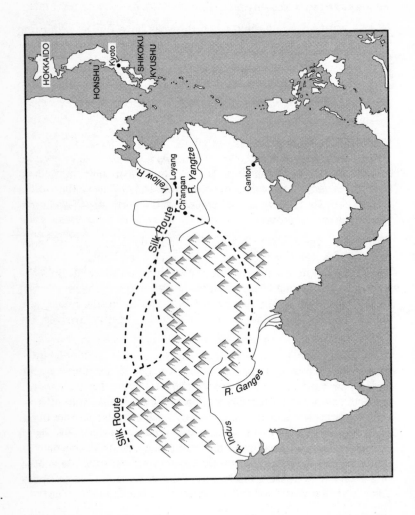

colonised Europe, Persia and India made it as far as Turkestan, in what is now north-west China, where they settled. Written records of theirs date back to the eighth century AD, when they were still using an Indo-European language (known as Tocharian), about 2,500 years after they first arrived there. The Chinese must have been in contact with these people, whose myths would have been similar to those of their fellow Aryans who settled the Indus valley.

Nevertheless, Chinese thought and culture do not seem to have been significantly influenced from outside, and the Chinese had their own, largely animistic, nature religion. Divination seems to have been important, as was human sacrifice and ancestor worship. The Chinese were – and still are – subject to earthquakes, floods, drought and crop failure, so it was important to try to bring these elements under their control.

The early Chinese believed in life after death, and in order to protect the souls of their ancestors they developed numerous burial and mourning rituals. Ancestor worship is still an important part of Chinese culture. These early Chinese believed that after the world was created, it was ruled over by a succession of twelve divine emperors, regarded as gods, each of whom reigned for 18,000 years.

As well as this early religion, there were three other religions that were, and still are, important in Chinese culture.

- **Confucianism** This is arguably more of a philosophy than a religion. It was developed by Kung Fu Tzu, known in the West as Confucius, who lived from 551 to 479 BC (he was a contemporary of the Buddha in India). At that time, China was not yet unified, and Confucius lived in the state of Lu in eastern China. He taught a strict code of ethics, and laid great emphasis on the principles of government, among other things. When China was finally unified in the late second century BC, the Confucians were the only ones who really understood how to run public affairs; consequently, they were appointed to senior posts and their philosophy gained currency. As time went on, later followers developed Confucianism into more of a religion – building temples, assimilating the ancient gods into their beliefs, and trying to deify Confucius himself (a move resisted by the Confucian scholars). Among the classic works said to be written or compiled by Confucius is the famous *I Ching*, or Book of Changes. Unfortunately, few early Confucian writings survive, since the first emperor of all China burned all books that were not about prophecy, farming or medicine, in 213 BC.

● **Taoism** After Confucius, there was a growth of philosophical thought. Where Confucius had been concerned chiefly with politics and ethics, other great thinkers began to ask questions of a deeper religious kind. They began to develop a philosophy which believed in the unity, or 'oneness' of everything; the Tao was 'the way', and the goal was to achieve perfect harmony with the universe. The great book of the Taoists is the *Tao Te Ching* ('the way and the power'), which is supposed to have been written by Lao Tzu, who was reputedly born in 604 BC. He may or may not have existed; scholars now think that the book is probably nothing to do with him. However, he became a central figure of the new religion and, once Buddhism arrived, he was deified like the Buddha, in rivalry.

● **Buddhism** This was, in fact, a heretical form of Hinduism, which started in India (where it subsequently died out almost entirely), and spread to China in the first or second century AD. It had grown popular enough to challenge the other two religions during the Tang dynasty (618 to 906 AD). Buddhism's central tenet is that through suffering and self-denial one can achieve enlightenment, a state of divine truth. When this happens, one is released from the cycle of death and rebirth; like the Hindus, the Buddhists believe in reincarnation. Buddhism was also more of a philosophy than a religion at first, but the Chinese turned it into a religion, in effect, and made the Buddha a god. It was through Buddhism more than anything else that Western mythology, and especially Indian mythology, influenced the Chinese.

What you have to remember is that China is a very big place. It's not so much a nation as a civilisation. Like India, it could accommodate a vast range of beliefs. So it managed to absorb all these philosophies, and blend them into a partially interlocking whole – rather like a three-part Venn diagram. And it overlaid them all with the mythology of its earlier beliefs. Some elements of Chinese mythology belong to two, or even all three, belief systems. At the same time, there are significant inconsistencies which the overall philosophy seems to accept quite comfortably. The result is an immensely rich and complex mythology.

The first real links with western culture came in the second century BC, when the Silk Route was first opened up. This trading route led from northern China, across the desert and steppe lands north of the

Himalayas, then through Persia and across to the Mediterranean. Although virtually no one would have travelled from one end to the other (there were frequent trading posts along the route), stories, myths and news would have travelled, with the goods, right the way through. Good stories would doubtless have been passed on, and those with particular appeal would sometimes have found their way into other mythologies. Although the famous Silk Route itself bypassed India entirely, there were other trading routes, overland and by sea, that linked China with India.

The purpose of the myths

It seems strange that all three of China's dominant belief systems started out merely as philosophies, yet all three became religions. It is presumably an indication of the importance of the old Chinese religion that it influenced all three of these later systems in this way. There also seems to be an inherent human desire to believe in supreme beings; why else would virtually every culture around the world have developed some kind of mythology that revolves around at least one god, if not many? Not only do people find these beliefs expedient to explain the natural world, they also need the security of an explanation that is bigger than them.

There was a marked division between the nobility and the ordinary people of China. The nobles and kings practised ancestor worship, with highly complex and detailed rituals when relatives die. Confucianism and Taoism were essentially their religions. The common people, however, were largely excluded from this tradition. They had sorcerers who helped them to placate evil spirits, for example, or to bring the rains, and their religion and mythology were much closer to the original Chinese beliefs.

Buddhism was far more accessible to the people than Confucianism or Taoism, although they adapted it to make the family more important than the individual, and a strong faith more important than self-denial. They also made karma transferable, so that someone else could choose to suffer on your behalf, to earn you spiritual credits to carry over into your next life. The Bodhisattvas were deified followers of the Buddha who achieved enlightenment but chose to remain on earth in order to save others in this way (in the same way that Jesus does in Christian mythology). This altruistic approach was new to the ordinary Chinese people, who welcomed it since they were not used to being on the receiving end of such generosity.

The myths of the Chinese reflect their admiration of hard work and of bravery, and there are many hero stories. There are also a number of myths in which the common people triumph over dictatorial rulers – an indication of the frequent struggle of the Chinese people against kings who did not have their interests at heart.

Gods and goddesses

The Chinese pantheon operates like a giant administrative bureaucracy – a reflection of the Chinese nation. There are departments containing strict hierarchies, which keep records and submit monthly reports to their department head. Once a year they report to the supreme god, who may promote or demote them, or even dismiss them, according to how well they have performed: a sort of divine appraisal system. This means that the gods may change. Old gods leave and new gods arrive. One of the reasons for this is that many of the gods started life as mortals and were subsequently deified, so the world of the gods necessarily functions much like the world of the mortals. This is presumably why virtually all of the Chinese deities are depicted in human form.

It also goes some way to explain why there is such a huge number of Chinese gods and goddesses. And not only are their ranks constantly being swelled, there are also local gods; every administrative area has its own (they are collectively called the gods of walls and ditches). In addition to this, some gods are important only in certain regions of China, so several gods may be performing the same function in different parts of the country.

This list includes the most important and popular gods, which are recognised throughout China. They are mostly Taoist gods, and many were absorbed from the earlier religion of the Chinese, from the days before Confucianism, Taoism and Buddhism. As well as these, there are countless weather gods, sea gods, sun and moon gods and so on, as well as gods for each profession.

Pan Gu   The first, creator-god, derived from the interaction of yin and yang, who formed the universe.

Nü Gua   Probably an ancient goddess, Nü Gua created the first people by moulding yellow clay. Eventually she got bored, dipped a rope into the yellow mud, and sprayed the drops around. The moulded clay figures became the Chinese nobility; the mud droplets became ordinary people. Nü Gua took care of the mortals, and saved them after the great flood (see page 107).

Fu Xi　The consort and (in some versions) brother of Nü Gua. In other versions he was the first emperor. He and Nü Gua were both usually depicted with snakes' tails. The snake was the totem, or clan symbol, of the Xia people who lived around 2000 BC, and these two may originally have been gods of theirs.

Zhu Rong　One of the next two gods to appear on earth after Nü Gua and Fu Xi. Zhu Rong was the god of fire.

Gong Gong　The god of water; once he and Zhu Rong arrive on earth, conflict begins (see page 106).

Jade Emperor (Yu-huang)　The supreme ruler of the heavens, often known as the August Personage of Jade. He is, in fact, the second of a triad of supreme rulers. Before him there was the Heavenly Master of the First Origin, and one day the Jade Emperor will be succeeded by the Heavenly Master of the Dawn of Jade of the Golden Door. He has daughters but no sons, since they might try to depose him.

Queen Mother of the West (Xi Wang Mu)　The wife of the Jade Emperor, she may originally have been a real person. She is an important figure in the Chinese pantheon, and she keeps the gods immortal by feeding them on the peaches of immortality, which ripen every 3,000 years. This is similar to the Viking goddess Idun, and could well have influenced her development – the trade routes between Europe and the Far East were well established by the time of the Vikings.

Lei-Kung　The thunder god, who is incredibly ugly. He is blue all over and has wings and claws. Lei-Kung punishes people who are guilty of terrible crimes, especially crimes that are outside the jurisdiction of human law, such as causing a death indirectly. He runs a whole department of lesser thunder gods.

T'ai-shan　Great Emperor of the Eastern Peak. He is the Jade Emperor's right-hand god when it comes to looking after humans. The Jade Emperor can't possibly find the time to deal directly with humans (apart from the Emperor of China himself), so he has delegated the job to T'ai-shan. T'ai-shan has a huge responsibility, and accordingly he has seventy-five departments under his control, each managed by a minor deity.

Sheng-mu   The Holy-mother. She is the daughter of the T'ai-shan, also known as the Princess of Streaked Clouds. She is a protector of women and children, and she also attends births.

Tsao-wang   The hearth god. He sees and hears everything that everyone in the family says and does. Every year, on the twenty-third day of the twelfth month, he goes up to heaven to give a report to the Jade Emperor. On the basis of the previous year's behaviour, the Jade Emperor allots each family good or bad luck for the coming year. During the one day of the year when Tsao-wang is in heaven, the members of the family can behave as they please since there is no witness.

Ts'ai-shen   The god of wealth, and one of the most popular gods. He runs a large department that includes such subordinate gods as the Immortal of Commercial Profits.

Wen Ch'ang   The god of literature has a number of gods under him, most notably the ugly god of examinations, who is more popular than he is, since he chooses who will come top in exams.

T'ien Hou   The Empress of Heaven (not to be confused with the Queen Mother of the West). She is associated with the sea and protects sailors.

Yen-wang   The god of death. The Chinese didn't have a hell until Buddhism arrived, but they made up for it afterwards, by devising the most complex hell imaginable. There are eighteen different hells, attached to ten law-courts. Yen-wang is head of the first law-court, where he judges the dead to decide which of the other law-courts they should be passed on to, according to the nature of their sins (they may be sent to more than one). The head of each law-court chooses which of the eighteen hells, each with a different type of punishment, are the most suitable to commit each soul to. Finally, the head of the tenth law-court is charged with making sure that the soul will fit properly into the body in which it is assigned to be reincarnated. Since the idea of hell came from India, it's not surprising that Yen-wang is, in fact, a form of the Vedic and Hindu god of death, Yama.

Ti-tsang Wang-p'u-sa   The Boddhisattva Ksitigarbha, a Buddhist deity who wanders through hell saving as many souls as he can by taking on their suffering.

Kuan Yin   The Bodhisattva Avalokita, or goddess of mercy. She was inherited, along with Buddhism, from India, where she was male. However, the Chinese associated her with the motherly quality of compassion, and made her female. She is depicted wearing a white veil and holding a child, and is in many ways reminiscent of the Christian Virgin Mary.

The Eight Immortals   These characters are central to Taoist mythology, where they set an example of how ordinary men and women can achieve enlightenment or, in mythological terms, immortality. Each of them was born mortal, and each became immortal by a different means: as a result of some selfless act of generosity, as the gift of a god, by following a great teacher, or through self-denial. They are often depicted holding peaches, the symbol of longevity.

The myth of creation

Needless to say, there are several creation myths. But by far the most important one is the story of Pan Gu. This dates from only the fourth century AD, although it may be somewhat older. However, only snippets of the earliest creation myths survive, apparently put together by several different authors, and the Pan Gu myth is by far the most comprehensive.

Parts of it seem strikingly similar to Indian mythology, with its idea of the cosmic egg, and Pan Gu holding up the world is reminiscent of Atlas in Greek myth. By the time this creation myth was developed, the trading routes between China and the Mediterranean had been open for 400 to 500 years, so it is quite possible that some elements of Western mythologies would have influenced the Chinese myths.

At the beginning, a primordial egg exists in the darkness; it is the product of the interaction of yin and yang, the two opposite, balancing forces of the universe. Inside the egg is Pan Gu, who has been asleep, growing, for 18,000 years. He suddenly wakes up, and is angry to find himself shut inside an egg, in total blackness.

In his rage, he flails about and cracks open the egg. And all the light parts of it float upwards to form the sky, while the heavy, opaque parts of it sink to form the earth. Pan Gu looks at this, and worries that the sky and earth won't stay where they are, but will merge together again. He decides that the only solution is for him to keep them apart by his own strength.

Pan Gu holds the sky with his head, and keeps the earth down with his feet, and then slowly begins to force the two apart. He has to grow 10 feet a day to keep up with them. Eventually, after 18,000 years, they are finally fixed in place.

Pan Gu is exhausted and lies down to die. His body becomes the mountains and valleys of the earth, his breath becomes wind and clouds, and his voice becomes thunder. His left eye is transformed into the sun and his right eye into the moon. His blood is the rivers and his sweat is rain and dew. The rest of his body forms everything else that is in the universe: stars, precious stones, metals, plants and trees. So Pan Gu both creates and becomes the universe and everything in it.

The myth of Zhu Rong and Gong Gong

This myth tells of the early gods who lived on the earth shortly after it was created. In an earlier part of the myths the goddess Nü Gua made the first humans; in this story she saves them. It's not hard to see, when you read it, that this is the mythologised history of a great earthquake and flood.

The Chinese were technologically advanced, and had a sophisticated understanding of the universe. By the first century AD, for example, Chinese mathematicians had calculated that the world must be round. This myth is another instance of the Chinese attempting to explain something that most of the rest of the world was not even aware of: the natural tilt of the earth.

The great god of water, Gong Gong, decides that he wants superiority over the god of fire, Zhu Rong. He attacks Zhu Rong in a huge chariot drawn by two terrifying dragons. He is followed by his two senior advisers, and an army of sea nymphs and underwater creatures.

But as they approach Zhu Rong, his dreadful heat starts to drive them back. They melt and burn, and eventually those that aren't killed run off, abandoning the fight. Gong Gong is so enraged that he rushes head first at the pillar which holds up the sky, the Imperfect Mountain, hitting it so hard that he collapses unconscious for a time. The pillar, meanwhile, cracks and crumbles. Great pieces fall from it and make huge holes in the ground.

Then the sky falls in. Huge holes appear in it, and everyone starts to run wildly in panic. Trees catch fire spontaneously, and huge cracks appear in the ground. Filthy water starts to gush from these cracks, which floods the land as it rushes towards the south-east of China, where the land has now become lower. This disruption throws the whole earth off balance, which is why the Pole Star is no longer directly overhead as it once was.

The goddess Nü Gua is worried about the people she created. So she collects different coloured pebbles from the river, and then smelts them in a furnace so she can mould them. She uses this mortar to fill in all the holes in the sky, and the gaping cracks in the ground. She is still not entirely sure that the sky will stay up, so she kills a giant turtle, cuts off its legs, and uses these to support the four corners of the sky. Finally, she stops the floods by taking reeds from the river-bed, burning them, and using the ashes to stop the gaps in the river-banks.

The myth of the silkworm goddess

Silk was important to the Chinese people; along with spices it was their most valuable product for trading with other peoples, along what was known as the Silk Route. The Chinese first began to spin silk in around 1200 BC; this myth tells how silk came to be.

A man and his daughter live together with their horse. The man is often away on business and his daughter misses him deeply. One day, when her father has been gone a long time, she is grooming the horse and talking to him. She tells him that she misses her father so much that she would marry anyone who brought him back to her.

The horse immediately bolts off and disappears in the distance. The next day, the man is busy doing business far away when his horse suddenly appears, neighing at him. The man is worried that something is wrong at home, so he jumps on the horse's back and heads home. When he arrives his daughter is delighted to see him; he asks her why the horse fetched him, and she replies that he must have known how much she missed her father.

The man is so impressed with his horse that he gives him extra fodder for the next few days. But the horse is off his food and behaving miserably, except when the daughter is nearby. Then he whinnies and rears up in excitement. After a few days the man begins to worry, and asks his daughter if she can explain the horse's strange behaviour. She remembers the remark she made to the horse about marrying anyone who brought her father home, so she tells her father about it.

He is furious at the horse's presumption in thinking that he could ever marry his daughter. Much as he admires the horse, that is going just too far. He is so angry that he goes out to the stable and kills the horse. Then he skins it, and hangs the skin up to dry in the sun.

The next day, the daughter is outside with some friends, and she sees the skin. She begins to taunt it when, suddenly, it flies up in the air and wraps itself round her. Then it carries her off out of sight of her friends. Her father comes home and he and his neighbours search for the girl. They find her at last, still wrapped in the horse's skin, at the top of a mulberry tree. She has turned into a worm-like creature, with a horse's head from which comes a continuous thread of white silk which she is slowly wrapping around herself.

This is how the daughter turned into the silkworm goddess, who later came down from heaven to give a present of silk to the Yellow Emperor. He was so delighted that he had new robes made from it, and his wife began to collect and cultivate silkworms. And that's how the Chinese people began to make silk.

Japan

Japanese civilisation started surprisingly late. We know relatively little about the original inhabitants of the Japanese islands, except that they practised some kind of animistic nature worship. These early tribes were invaded by by the shamanistic people of north-east Asia, who crossed the Korean straits in the fourth century AD. These people believed that the world was inhabited by good and evil spirits who could be controlled only by the tribal shaman, or medicine man.

These invaders drove the aboriginal Ainu tribe into the north of Japan, and defeated the tribes further south. They gradually assimilated these tribes and their beliefs into their own culture. However, they were still essentially a disunited collection of clans, who now followed broadly the same religion, known as Shinto (meaning 'the way of the gods').

Until the sixth century AD, these people kept no written records of their beliefs, since they had not yet developed writing. But at the start of the sixth century several things happened.

For one thing, one of the Japanese clans – known as the Yamato – managed to achieve superiority over the others. This was important to Japanese mythology because each clan had its own ancestors who had achieved divine status; from this point on, it was the Yamato clan whose myths became the national focus. (It is this clan whose direct descendants are the present-day Japanese emperors.)

The next thing that happened was that the king of Korea decided it would be politic to make a goodwill gesture towards the new emperor of Japan. So in 552 AD he sent him some Buddhist missionaries. Buddhism became immediately popular in Japan, although it didn't displace Shinto but existed alongside it.

And the third important thing that happened was that the Buddhist missionaries brought something with them: the art of writing. The Japanese quickly adapted the Chinese system of writing to create their own variant, and from that point on they began to record their religious beliefs.

Buddhism and Shinto borrowed extensively from one another in Japan, although they retained their own identities. This meant that Shinto was being influenced by both the Chinese and the Indian thought behind Buddhism. It is difficult to tell precisely how strong this influence was, however, because of the absence of records of Shinto before the arrival of Buddhism. What's more, Shinto never became a fully unified religion because of the tribal nature of the Japanese way of life.

The purpose of the myths

The followers of Shinto worship Kami, or divine forces of nature. The Kami are anthropomorphic – in other words they have human form and actions – and they each possess two souls; one gentle and one aggressive. They are not omniscient; some of them live in heaven and some on earth, and they have to send messengers between them to find out what is happening in their absence.

The Japanese traditionally led a rural life until comparatively recently, and their gods are gods of sun, moon, stars, rain, rice and so on – nothing like the Chinese gods of professions and exams.

The Japanese heaven is like Japan, but even more beautiful. It is relatively nearby and used to be linked to Japan by a sort of bridge so that the gods could move between heaven and earth. This supposedly collapsed one day when the gods were asleep; the result is the isthmus to the west of Kyoto. This straightforward, unbureaucratic view also indicates the simple lifestyle of the Japanese people. Until the arrival of Buddhism the Shinto afterlife was a shadowy place, but it didn't include any notion of punishment. This attitude to death is usually (though not invariably) found in the mythologies of less sophisticated cultures. The Buddhist beliefs influenced Shinto, of course, and some Shinto myths subsequently acquired more hellish overtones, such as the Shinto myth of Izanagi and Izanami (see page 113).

A significant number of the Kami of Shinto mythology are gods and goddesses of storms and wind, and of mountains (which include volcanoes); this reflects the violent natural forces that the Japanese have to contend with. Interestingly, there is no record of a god of earthquakes until the year 599 AD, shortly after a particularly violent earthquake. The cult of Nai-no-Kami began, and over the years several sanctuaries were dedicated to him.

The chief deity in the Shinto pantheon is Amaterasu, the goddess of the sun. The myth in which she hides her light from the earth (page 115) refers to an actual event, although scholars cannot agree on whether it is an eclipse, or the onset of winter.

Gods and goddesses

There are numerous gods and goddesses, and their roles are not always clear since the myths about them vary from place to place, and between various early written versions.

Izanagi　The first god of earth, who created the world. Father of Amaterasu, Tsuki-yomi and Susano.

Izanami　The first goddess of earth, wife of Izanagi.

Kagu-Zuchi　The fire god, also worshipped under the name of Ho-Masubi, meaning causer of fire. The last child of Izanagi and Izanami, whose birth killed his mother. During the windy season the Japanese wooden houses were prone to being destroyed by fire, so it was important to keep Ho-Masubi placated with rituals.

Amaterasu　The sun goddess and ruler of heaven.

Tsuki-yomi　Amaterasu's brother, god of the moon.

Susano　Wicked storm god and brother of Amaterasu.

Wakahiru-me　Younger sister of Amaterasu, and probably a goddess of the rising sun.

Kusa-nada-hime　The 'Rice Paddy Princess' and wife of Susano.

O-Kuni-Nushi　The god of medicine and sorcery, and son of Susano.

Ame-no-Oshido-Mimi　Son of Amaterasu, sent by her to control the earth, but he refused to go because it was too full of disturbances.

Ninigi　Grandson of Amaterasu, finally sent by her to reign over the earth.

Kono-Hana-Sukuya-Hime　Daughter of a mountain god and wife of Ninigi.

Takami-Musubi　One of Amaterasu's chief assistants.

Amo no Uzume　Another solar deity, thought to be the goddess of the dawn.

Inari　The rice god and god of prosperity.

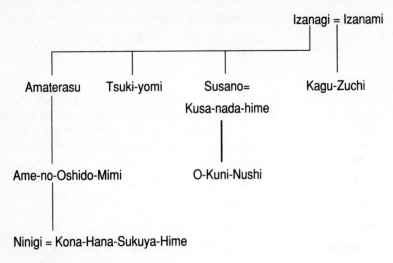

The Japanese pantheon

The creation myth

> Although this purports to be the Shinto myth of creation, the start of it owes a great deal to the influence of Chinese and Indian mythology, as you'll see. However, it is clear when you read it that it is the myth of an island people.

To begin with, there is nothing but a shapeless egg. Gradually, the lighter, clearer part rises up to become the heavens, and the denser, opaque part sinks to become the earth. Three gods are created 'of themselves', who go and hide high up in heaven.

The earth is still not solid, and pieces of land are floating about on it. Then an object appears, floating between heaven and earth, which looks like the first shoot of a new reed. Two gods are born from this, who also hide. Seven more generations of gods are born this way, and the last pair are Izanagi and Izanami.

These two stand on the 'floating bridge of heaven' and wonder whether there is anything down below. So they take the jewelled spear of heaven and dip the end of it into the sea below, to see if there is anything there. When they bring it back up, a drop has formed on its point, which falls to the sea and becomes the island of Onokoro. Izanagi and Izanami now have somewhere to live, and they go down to the island. They stick the spear in the ground to form a heavenly pillar.

They decide to produce children to form more islands, so they devise themselves a marriage ritual. They set out to walk round the column in opposite directions. When they meet, Izanami says, 'How wonderful!' I've met a handsome young man!" Then they have sexual intercourse. They have agreed how they will do this, because they have discovered that Izanami's body is improperly formed at a corresponding point to where Izanagi's is overly formed; they decided the best idea would be to bring these two parts of their bodies together. This seems to work, and Izanami gives birth.

But instead of producing an island, as they had hoped, Izanami produces a deformed leech-child. They put this child into a reed boat and cast it adrift. (There is an old Japanese ritual that involves making a clay figure when a first child is born, and casting the model adrift in a reed boat as a scapegoat). Izanagi and Izanami go to consult the gods on where they have gone wrong. The gods explain that it was all Izanami's fault, because she was the first to speak when the two of them met round the pillar. It is not the woman's place, the gods explain, to speak first. If they want proper children, they'll have to try again, and this time Izanagi will have to open the conversation.

The two gods return to earth, and try again. This time, everything goes according to plan and Izanami gives birth to all the islands of Japan. She and Izanagi decide that they will create gods to beautify their islands. So they create numerous gods – of wind, trees, rivers and mountains – and the creation of the islands is completed.

The myth of Izanagi and Izanami

This myth continues the story of these two gods after they finished creating Japan. It is particularly interesting for its parallel with the Greek myth of Demeter and Persephone – it is another food of the dead myth – although its ending is different. It is even more similar to another Greek myth, Orpheus and Eurydice, in which Orpheus is told he can have his wife back from the underworld on the condition that he doesn't look over his shoulder on the way out to check that she is following. He succumbs to the temptation, looks back, and loses her for ever.

It is quite likely that the Buddhists would have come across the Greek myth (trade between East and West had been flourishing for centuries). Since the more hellish overtones of this story are undoubtedly a Buddhist invention, it's possible that they also contributed some elements of the plot, perhaps borrowed from the Greek.

The last child that Izanami produces is the god of fire. This god's birth burns her genitals so badly that she dies. As she dies, however, she continues to produce gods, from her urine, her excrement and her vomit. Izanagi is so angry that he cuts the fire god's head off; drops of his blood give birth to still more deities.

Izanagi is so miserable at losing Izanami that he decides to travel to Yomi, the underworld, to try to bring her back to life. When he eventually arrives at the gates of the underworld, after a long journey, Izanami meets him. He cannot even see her properly since the place is so dark and shadowy, but he tells her how much he loves her and how he wants her to come back with him. She tells him off, however, for taking so long to arrive. She says she isn't allowed to go back with him now, because she has eaten the food of Yomi.

Eventually, he persuades her to discuss the matter with the gods of hell. But she makes him promise that he won't try to follow her into the underworld and look at her. He agrees, but then he cannot resist the thought of what might be his last ever sight of his beloved wife. So he breaks a tooth off his comb and uses it as a torch. He steps into the underworld, only to find Izanami's body lying there, rotting and riddled with maggots. He is so horrified he runs back towards the earth.

Izanami rises and screams after him that he has humiliated her. She sends the hags of hell after him, with eight thunder gods. Izanagi reaches the end of the path from hell and picks three peaches from a tree; he drives his pursuers back by hurling the peaches at them. Then he blocks the entrance to the underworld with a huge boulder, just as Izanami arrives at the other side of it.

They speak to each other from opposite sides of the great rock.

Izanami tells Izanagi that he must accept her death. He recognises this and agrees not to try to visit her again. Then they formally declare their marriage ended.

After this, Izanagi is exhausted and decides to cleanse and refresh himself by bathing in a stream. Various gods and goddesses are born from his clothes as he takes them off, from his stick as he puts it down, and from his body while he is bathing. Finally he produces the sun goddess, Amaterasu, when he washes his left eye, the moon god Tsuki-yomi from his right eye, and the storm god Susano from his nose.

Izanagi decides to divide his world between these three children. He instructs Amaterasu to rule heaven, Tsuki-yomi to rule the night, and Susano to rule the seas. Amaterasu and Tsuki-yomi agree, but Susano complains that he would rather go to the land of his dead mother. Izanagi is angry and banishes Susano. Then he withdraws from the world and goes to live in high heaven.

The myth of Amaterasu hiding the sun

This myth is about the row between Amaterasu and her brother, which many historians believe is an account of the war between two tribes early in Japan's history. It is also a cosmic myth, since it attempts to explain the disappearance of the sun.

When Izanagi banishes Susano, Susano announces that he wants to go up to heaven and say goodbye to his sister Amaterasu before he goes. She is suspicious of his intentions, and arms herself with a bow and arrows when she goes to meet him.

Susano tells her that she has nothing to fear from him, and suggests that he give her proof of his good faith. He proposes that both of them create children, and that he will produce male children to prove his sincerity. Amaterasu agrees, and asks her brother for his sword. He gives it to her and she breaks it into three. She crunches each part in her mouth, and her breath gives birth to three goddesses.

Then Susano asks for Amaterasu's five strings of beads from around her neck. He crunches them up and breathes out five gods.

Amaterasu claims that these gods are her children, since they were created from her beads. But Susano disagrees, and claims he has won a great victory. Then he starts to celebrate by breaking down the walls of the rice fields, blocking in the irrigation channels and defecating in the temple where the festival of the first fruits, or harvest festival, is due to be held shortly.

One of Amaterasu's duties is to weave clothes for the gods. One day she is sitting in the weaving hall with her women when Susano throws a flayed horse through the roof. This is so terrifying that one of the women pricks herself with a needle and dies. Amaterasu is so frightened she runs away and hides in a cave. She blocks the entrance with a huge boulder. Without the sun goddess, the world is plunged into darkness.

Chaos follows, the rice fields lie fallow and the wicked gods revel in the secrecy which the darkness affords them, and behave worse than ever. An assembly of 800 myriad gods meets to discuss how to coax Amaterasu out of hiding, and they come up with a plan.

First they set up a magical mirror outside the cave. Then they collect roosters, to crow outside the cave. Next, they persuade the goddess of the dawn, Amo no Uzume, to dance on an upturned barrel outside the cave, drumming with her feet. As she becomes more carried away, she takes her clothes off, and the gods start to laugh uproariously.

As the gods intended, Amaterasu peeks out to ask what on earth is going on. The gods tell her that they are celebrating because they have found an even better goddess than her. She comes out of the cave, and sees her own reflection in the magic mirror. The gods block the cave behind her so she can't go back into hiding, and they have their sun back.

The 800 myriad gods punish Susano by fining him, cutting off his beard and moustache, tearing out his fingernails and toenails, and expelling him from heaven.

5

AMERICAN MYTHOLOGY

—— North America: The Iroquois ——

When you study their mythology, you can see the similarities between the native Americans and the Mongolians and Siberians of north-east Asia, who crossed to Alaska over the Bering straits when there was still a land bridge there (these were the same race that the Japanese Ainu were descended from). This migration to America may have started as long ago as 60,000 years. There were probably intermittent waves of settlers after that – once people began to make rafts and boats, the Bering Straits weren't hard to cross.

But the next big wave of immigrants came in the thirteenth century AD when several nomadic tribes arrived from north-east Asia, escaping from Genghis Khan and his Mongol Hordes. These tribes spread out down the west side of America and across Canada, and became the Apache and Navaho peoples.

The closest similarity between the people of Siberia and north-east Asia and the native Americans is the shamanistic nature of their religions. Their medicine-men or medicine-women are intermediaries between the world of humans and the world of spirits. By going into a trance state they can communicate with the spirits, and direct them to act in a certain way. For example, they can instruct the spirit of an illness to leave a sick person, or the spirit of the mountain lion to accompany the hunters and give them help. In some cases this trance is induced with the help of natural hallucinogens, especially peyote

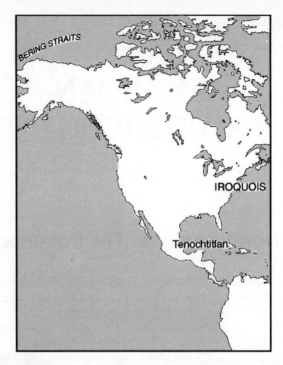

which is derived from a particular type of cactus. Shamans are different from priests because they are not merely a voicebox for the gods, or an intercessor; they actually possess and wield power over the spirits.

The native Americans finally lost their relatively undisturbed hold on their continent when the Europeans arrived in the seventeenth century. For 200 years they fought a losing battle against the superior weapons of the Europeans, until the last great battle when the Sioux were massacred at Wounded Knee Creek by the US cavalry in 1890.

When the Europeans arrived in the sixteenth and seventeenth centuries there were 2,000 independent tribes in north America (of which only 300 remain, living on reserves). They divide broadly into ten groups of tribes, each with its own language, although all these languages are loosely related. So the Iroquois race, for example, consisted of a number of independent tribes. The other main groups, or ethnic divisions, were the Athapascans, the Algonquins, the Salish, the Californians, the Pimas, the Shoshoneans, the Sioux, the Caddoans and the Muskhogeans.

One of the biggest disadvantages the native Americans had in beating off the new invasion was that they were so disunited; they were far more interested in fighting among themselves than in banding together to fight the common enemy.

One of the few exceptions to this was among the Iroquois-speaking tribes, who occupied land to the east and north-east of the Great Lakes, and down to what is now New York. Several of these tribes managed to form a group known as the Five Nations Confederacy (consisting of the Mohawk, Onondaga, Oneida, Cayuga and Seneca tribes). These people were involved in many of the early colonial wars, and this unity gave them a huge advantage when defending their land against the European colonisers.

The purpose of the myths

The Iroquois, like all the native Americans, performed rites and rituals to placate the gods, or spirits, and to persuade them to give their protection and help. Many of these rituals were complex and long lasting, and could involve mass dances that went on for several days. The rituals would often be focused on the totem pole, a tall wooden post decorated with carvings and paintings of the tribal totems.

The myths themselves were crucial in binding the tribe together, since tribal identity was important to the native Americans. They also served to explain the history of the race and the forces of nature, and to set examples for human behaviour; many of them, for example, demonstrate how to treat animals with respect.

The Iroquois had a number of heroes – almost certainly based in fact – whom they wove myths around, particularly later on in their history. The two most important of these were Atotarho and Hiawatha. Atotarho was a hugely successful warrior of the Onondaga tribe, whose tribal costume was made with snakeskins. These were considered very magical and, as a result, Atotarho came to be seen as a sorcerer of immense power, and an example of courage and strength.

Hiawatha represented different qualities – he was a peacemaker. According to the Iroquois (and this is probably true in essence), it was Hiawatha who engineered the setting up of the Five Nations Confederacy. He was either a Mohawk or an Onondaga and he persuaded the chiefs of all the tribes (including Atotarho, who was his contemporary) to stop the bloodshed and rally together. Longfellow's famous poem *Hiawatha*, by the way, tells an entirely different story which is not Iroquois but Algonquin. Longfellow simply borrowed Hiawatha's name from the Iroquois to give to his hero.

The gods and goddesses

The Iroquois pantheon has many characters who are animistic spirits of animals or forces of nature. So myths will contain Sun and Moon, for example, who are personifications of the sun and moon, and no more. Some characters, however, are drawn in more detail, and the most important are listed here.

The Iroquois myths are also full of dwarves, giants and dragons, and monsters that are like huge, exaggerated and terrifying versions of bears and other native animals.

Atahensic   The sky goddess who fell to earth at the beginning of creation.

Breath of Wind   Atahensic's daughter, and mother of Ioskeha and Tawiscara.

Master of Winds   God of the winds and father of Ioskeha and Tawiscara.

Ioskeha   Creator of the first man and woman.

Tawiscara   The twin brother, or evil aspect, of Ioskeha.

Hino the Thunder Spirit   The guardian of the sky, who equates with the thunderbird of other native American races. He has a bow, and arrows of fire. He killed the water serpent who lived in the Great Lakes, and destroyed the stone giants of the west.

Rainbow   The wife of Hino.

Echo   Together with Wind and Thunder, one of the three most important gods.

Gunnodoyak   A young hunter who was once mortal but who was adopted by Hino, and almost killed by the water serpent. Hino revived him, however, and took him back up to heaven with him.

Oshadagea   An eagle who attends Hino and lives in the Western sky. He carries a lake of dew in the hollow of his back, which he sprinkles over the earth to revive it whenever the fire spirits burn all the vegetation.

Keneu   A golden eagle, and Hino's other constant attendant.

Eithinoha   The earth, whose name means 'our mother'.

Onatha   The Spirit of Wheat and Eithinoha's daughter. In a classic fertility myth, she went looking for dew one morning and was abducted by the Spirit of Evil who imprisoned her under the ground with him until the Sun found her and brought her back to the fields.

The creation myth

This creation story is similar among all the Iroquois nations. It also contains elements which are reminiscent of the Japanese creation myth. It's impossible to know for certain whether the two myths are related at all, but America and Japan were both originally settled by the people of north-east Asia.

This myth contains a common theme, that of twin brothers, one of whom is good and the other evil. In common with Romulus and Remus, and Cain and Abel, these brothers represent the two sides of human nature.

Above the sky, there is another world that is like this one, and which has always been there. At the start, there is only water in the world below, and in it are animals that know how to swim.

The sky chief has a daughter called Atahensic. When she grows up she sets out across the land of the 'chief who owns the earth' whom she is going to marry. After a dangerous journey she reaches his hut, which is next to the great tree of heaven, and marries him. But when she becomes pregnant, he is overcome with great jealousy and mistrust of her. At length she produces a daughter, called Breath of Wind. But her husband is so jealous by now that he uproots the tree of heaven and flings his wife and child into the abyss that is created where the roots once were.

Atahensic falls through the sky and sees that there is a huge lake below her, but no land. Meanwhile, the animals in the water have seen her falling towards them and they decide they had better create some earth for her to land on. The musk rat fetches earth from the bed of the lake and brings it to the surface on the turtle's back. As soon as the earth reaches the surface it becomes huge and solid, and becomes the land. Birds come and support Atahensic on their backs, and set her down gently on the new earth.

Breath of Wind grows up and is visited one night by the Master of Winds. She gives birth to twins, Ioskeha and Tawiscara. They hate each other so much that even before they are born they start to fight, and cause their mother's death as a result. Atahensic makes the sun and the moon from her daughter's body, but she doesn't put them in the sky. The evil Tawiscara convinces Atahensic that it was his brother alone who had caused Breath of Wind's death. So Atahensic banishes Ioskeha.

Ioskeha goes to see his father, Master of Winds, who gives him both maize and a bow and arrows. He is now master of hunting and farming. Ioskeha then creates land animals, and learns the secrets of medicine and tobacco from Hadui, the dwarf and bringer of diseases, whom he defeats. Next, he steals the sun and moon from his grandmother Atahensic and sets them on their courses in the sky. Then he models the first man and the first woman from the mud.

Tawiscara, Ioskeha's evil twin, tries to imitate him but he can only create fierce creatures. In the end Ioskeha defeats him and sends him away; he goes to live in the far north-west, where he rules the land where the souls of the dead live.

The myth of the invention of medicine

In this story, the totemic nature of the native American gods is much in evidence. Each of the groups of animals that meets is a tribe, symbolised by its animal totem. The decision made by the meeting of the smaller animals is probably a reference to the fact that huge numbers of native Americans were killed by diseases introduced to North America by European invaders.

In the beginning, the animals have the gift of speech and live happily alongside humans. But people multiply so quickly that the animals are forced to go away and live where there is more space, in the forests and deserts. Soon the friendship between animals and humans becomes a thing of the past. As time goes on, people invent lethal weapons and begin to kill animals for their skins and their meat.

The animals grow angry about this, and decide to do something about it. The bear tribe meet together to discuss it, led by their chief, Old White Bear. They want to declare war but, having no weapons of their own, they realise that this would be foolish. So they decide to make a bow and arrow that they can use against humans. They find a curved piece of wood, and one of the bears sacrifices himself so that his fellow bears can use his gut to string the bow. But when the bow is finally made, the bears find that they cannot use it properly because their claws get in the way. One bear cuts his claws, but Old White Bear points out that they can't all do this, or they wouldn't be able to climb trees or catch game, and then the whole tribe would starve.

Meanwhile, the deer are also meeting under the leadership of their chief, Little Deer. They decide that if any human kills a deer without asking for forgiveness with due respect, they should be struck down with rheumatism. They pass this decision on to the local tribe of Indians, and tell them how to ask for pardon properly if they are ever driven to kill a deer.

Whenever a deer is killed, Little Deer runs to the body and asks the spirit of the deer whether the hunter asked for forgiveness properly. If the answer is no, Little Deer finds the hunter and causes him to have crippling rheumatism.

Next, the fish and the reptiles decide that if they are hunted by humans, they will visit them with nightmares of snakes wrapping themselves around them, and of eating rotten fish. All the other animals – the birds and insects and spiders and grubs – meet and invent numerous diseases with which they will punish any humans who harm them without good cause.

But the plants, which were still on friendly terms with humans, overhear the animals' plans and decide to do what they can to help. Every tree, grass and flower decides that it will provide a remedy for some of the diseases that the smaller animals have invented. The medicine doctor can use these to cure his tribe members' illnesses and, if he is in doubt as to what remedy to use, the spirit of the plant will advise him.

The myth of Sayadio's visit to the land of spirits

This story is similar to the Greek story of Orpheus and Eurydice in particular, and to other myths of travels through the underworld in search of someone who has died, like the Japanese story of Izanagi and Izanami. What is interesting is that in this version – the most primitive and animistic – Sayadio has physically to reunite the spirit and the body. The Japanese myth refers to this separation indirectly, when Izanagi speaks with his wife and then sees her body rotting and crawling with maggots. The Greek myth, however, makes no reference to it at all.

These myths – like the story of Gilgamesh – all carry the message that you cannot conquer death, however close you may come to doing so (and Sayadio comes frustratingly close to succeeding).

Sayadio is desperately upset at the death of his young sister, and decides that he wants her back so badly that he will go and look for her in the land of spirits. He spends years searching hopelessly, and then he meets an old man who gives him a magic hollow gourd. This old man tells him that if he finds his sister, he can catch her spirit in the gourd.

Sayadio feels more optimistic after this, and continues his journey. After a time he reaches the land of spirits. He expects the spirits to come and greet him but, to his surprise, they run away terrified. He is somewhat put out by this, and goes to speak to the spirit master of ceremonies, who tells him that the spirits are gathering to celebrate a dance festival, just as the Indians do during their lives.

The dance begins, and the spirits float round mistily. He sees his sister and leaps forwards to catch her, but she dissolves through his fingers. The master of ceremonies feels sorry for Sayadio, and gives him a magic rattle which, when shaken, will make Sayadio's sister come back. He rattles it, and sees his sister again among the spirit dancers. She is so absorbed in the music that she takes no notice of him. But

Sayadio takes out the gourd and in a flash he has caught his sister's spirit and put the cover back on the gourd before she can escape from it.

Delighted with his success, Sayadio rushes home to his village. He calls his friends together to witness him bringing his sister back to life. Her body is brought out and everything is prepared, when a thoughtless young woman decides that she wants to know what a disembodied spirit looks like, so she takes the lid off the gourd to have a look.

Immediately the spirit of Sayadio's sister flies out, and back to the land of spirits. When Sayadio realises what has happened his heart breaks and he falls to the ground and dies.

Mexico

Some of the north-east Asians who migrated to north America moved right down the continent. By 9000 BC they had made it all the way to South America. Several tribes settled in Central America, and in the area that is now Mexico.

Although these tribes were often at war with each other, they possessed a certain unity of culture and beliefs. Like the north Americans, their culture was shamanic. Of the important tribes of this region, the earliest were the Olmecs, whose culture flourished from about 1500 to 400 BC. By about 300 AD the Zapotecs and the Mayans had risen to prominence, to be followed in around 900 AD by the Toltecs, who settled in the central Mexican plateau at around the same time as the Nahua who were their chief rivals, as the later myths of the Aztects indicated (see the myth of Tezcatlipoca and Quetzalcoatl on page 130).

The Toltec civilisation collapsed at the end of the twelfth century AD as a result of civil war, and was replaced about fifty years later by the Aztecs, who were descended from the Nahua. This warring and violent tribe were also highly organised, civilised in many ways, and had a great respect for music and the arts. They had enormous admiration for the Toltecs and their gods, whom they absorbed into their pantheon and revered highly.

Central America is highly prone to hurricanes, earthquakes and floods, and this unstable and often violent existence is reflected in the Aztecs' beliefs. They seemed to live as if they had little time left, which is what they believed (they thought the world was already into extra time and couldn't last much longer); their outlook was very pessimistic. They believed, for example, that they could earn a better afterlife if they confessed and were absolved of their sins. But they could do this only once, so they tried to time it accurately so they would confess at the very last minute. The priest or shaman would then set them a penance, such as fasting, which would probably finish them off. If it didn't, they couldn't afford to commit any more sins. Even if they got their timing perfect, they had only won eternal blackness in Mictlan, the underworld. But at least they had avoided the violent punishments that waited for those people who had not confessed in time.

The Aztec centre was at Tenochtitlan, an extraordinary city built on an island in the middle of a lake (on the site of the present-day Mexico City). Tenochtitlan had a population of around 200,000 and covered 5 square miles, intersected by canals – rather like Venice – and linked to the mainland by causeways. Even the Spanish, who conquered the Aztecs in 1521, were astounded by its design.

The purpose of the myths

Many of the Aztec myths revolve around their particularly bloody and violent obsession with human sacrifice. This was necessary, they believed, in order to keep the world alive (see the creation myth, on page 128). To this end, they captured all the prisoners they could from neighbouring tribes so that they had a ready supply of sacrificial victims without having to draw on their own population.

Every deity in their pantheon was associated with a compass direction, and they had a hugely complex calendar which had a religious as well as a practical function; it was used for divination. It combined the 365 days of the solar year with a 260-day sacred calendar. This meant that the entire cycle lasted 52 years, made up of 18,980 days, each with a unique date.

The gods and goddesses

There were numerous Aztec gods, not least because the Aztecs believed it was a sign of respect to take over the gods of the tribes they conquered, so they had to keep adding more deities to their pantheon. They paid these gods huge honour, unlike the way that most peoples treat conquered gods, although they were of course not that distantly related to their neighbouring tribes. This meant, among other things, that they were quite likely to end up with several gods whose functions overlapped.

Ometecuhtli, the dual god – both male and female – was the first creator.

Huitzilopochtli (hummingbird of the south) was the Aztecs' totemic tribal god, who was both the sun-god and the god of warriors.

Tezcatlipoca (smoking mirror) was a creator-god, and the supreme god of the Aztec pantheon, associated with the night, the moon and destruction.

Quetzalcoatl (feathered serpent) was another creator, and god of the morning and evening star. He was also worshipped as the god of the wind, under the name Ehecatl. Originally he was a Toltec god.

Tlaloc was an earlier god of the Olmec people, whom they worshipped as an animistic jaguar deity. He was a god of rain who made things grow or, if he rained too hard, made them rot. Every year the priests sacrificed newborn babies to him; the more they cried, the better the omen, since their tears symbolised the rain that would fall.

Chalchiuhtlicue was the wife (or sometimes sister) of Tlaloc and the goddess of running water. She also functioned as a fertility goddess, causing the crops to grow, and was associated with marriage. She was often invoked to protect newborn babies, presumably because it was thought she had some influence with her husband Tlaloc.

Tlazolteotl was an earth goddess and fertility goddess who came to represent sexual guilt, lust and filth.

Xipe Totec (the flayed lord) was a god of vegetation, particularly of planting. Sacrificial victims were flayed and the priest would wear the skin.

Huehueteotl, the god of fire, was the oldest god in the pantheon, whose worship may have dated back as far as 1500 BC.

Chicomecoatl was the female aspect of the corn, and therefore the goddess of plenty (like the Roman Ceres). Her sacrificial victim – also flayed – would be a young girl.

Cinteotl (maize cob lord) was the male aspect of the corn, particularly associated with maize.

Xochiquetzal (feather flower) was responsible for fertility and childbirth, flowers, and singing and dancing. She was also the goddess of weavers.

Xochipili was the brother, and sometimes the illicit consort, of Xochiquetzal, who was associated with the corn gods Xipe Totec and Cinteotl.

Mictlantecuhtli was the ruler – and creator – of the underworld, Mictlan.

Mictecacihuatl, his wife, helped Mictlantecuhtli to govern the nine layers of the underworld and its nine rivers.

The creation myth

The Aztecs believed that there was a cycle of creation, and the world was created and destroyed five times (this is the fifth world). The manner in which the fifth world was created is the Aztec's reason for believing that the life of the world could be perpetuated only through sacrifice. Even so, the fifth and final world would also be destroyed in the end, by earthquakes.

At the very beginning, there is Ometecuhtli, who is both male and female. He exists outside time and space, and represents all dualities: chaos and order, dark and light, evil and goodness. This 'lord of duality' creates Tezcatlipoca, Xipe Totec, Huitzilopochtli and Quetzalcoatl. He then creates Tlaloc and his consort Chalchiuhtlicue.

These gods then go on to create five successive worlds, each with its own sun. The first world is lit by the earth sun, but its people behave badly and the gods destroy them by sending jaguars to eat them. The second world, lit by the air sun, is inhabited by people devoid of wisdom, so the gods punish them by sending hurricanes which turn them all into apes.

The people of the third world, lit by the fiery sun, have no respect for the gods so they are destroyed by all manner of fires and volcanoes. The sun of water lights the fourth world, whose people are made from the ash of the third world. They are drowned as a punishment for being so greedy.

This world is the fifth world. Before they create it the gods meet to discuss who will create its sun – a sun that will combine the elements of the four previous suns: earth, air, fire and water. This will be the four-movement sun. A wealthy god, dressed in a lavish costume, steps forward and volunteers. The other gods say that one god will not be enough, and they ask Nanautzin to help. Nanautzin is ugly and disfigured and covered in sores, and the other gods have always ignored him in the past, so he is surprised to be asked; but he agrees to help.

The two gods purify the sacrificial fire and make offerings. The wealthy god lays gold and precious jewels on the fire, but all Nanautzin can manage is some reeds and some hay, thorns covered in his blood, and the scabs from his sores. Then the other gods tell the wealthy god that he must jump into the fire and sacrifice himself to create the new sun.

The god cannot bring himself to jump into the flames, and backs away in shame. But Nanautzin has the courage to do it, and leaps on to the burning pyre, giving life to the sun. The cowardly god is so mortified that he manages to throw himself in after Nanautzin, but it is Nanautzin who is honoured afterwards among the gods.

Now the fifth world has been created, Quetzalcoatl and Tezcatlipoca look down from heaven and see only water below them. But a huge goddess is floating on the water, eating everything in it. The two gods decide that there's no point creating anything unless they get rid of her first, or she'll just eat whatever they create. So they turn themselves into huge serpents and grab her – one by her arms and the other by her legs – and pull her in half. Then they use her head and shoulders to create the earth, and the rest of her body to form the sky.

When they hear about it, the other gods are not impressed at this treatment of the goddess. They decide to compensate her for what has happened, so they create trees and plants, caves and rivers, mountains and valleys from her body. They agree that she will provide whatever humans need for survival.

Quetzalcoatl tricks the lord of the underworld, Mictlantecuhtli, into giving him the bones of a man and woman from an earlier world. He grinds these into dust and then mixes them with his own blood. He moulds this mixture into men and women to populate the new earth.

But the goddess is still unhappy at the way she has been treated. Sometimes she cries, and refuses to give the humans what they need until she has been fed on human blood. She sustains human life, so human life must sustain her.

The myth of Tezcatlipoca and Quetzalcoatl

Tezcatlipoca was the dark god of destructive forces, and Quetzalcoatl was the light god; the two of them were in constant rivalry. This myth was a reference to the fact that Tezcatlipoca was originally the god of the Nahua tribes (from whom the Aztecs were descended). The Nahua were at war with the Toltecs, whose gods included Quetzalcoatl. The stories below are taken from the tales of Tezcatlipoca's efforts to bring down the Toltec city of Tollan (the modern city of Tula).

Although Tezcatlipoca is killed at the end of this story, it is not a permanent death. The Aztecs, in any case, believed that all their gods died each night, were reduced to bones, and then returned every morning.

At the end of the rivalry between the two gods, Quetzalcoatl was so worn down by the fight that he resolved to leave Tollan, and he set off on a raft made of serpents, and headed out across the sea to the east, where he became the evening star – the planet Venus. There was a prophecy (not unlike the British story of King Arthur) that one day Quetzalcoatl would return over the sea from the east to claim his kingdom – an idea which terrified the Aztecs. The Spanish conqueror Cortes exploited this when he reached Mexico in 1519; the Aztec ruler Montezuma thought that Cortes was Quetzalcoatl, and the Spaniard did nothing to disillusion him.

Tezcatlipoca is jealous of the abundant, successful state of the Toltec people, and decides to bring about the downfall of their chief city, Tollan. He announces a great feast in the city which everyone is invited to. Everyone dances and sings, and Tezcatlipoca begins to sing to them all. He makes them keep time for him with their feet, and he gradually speeds up the song, until the pace of their dancing becomes so furious that they are driven mad. Large numbers of them lose their footing and fall into a deep ravine, where they are turned into rocks and stones.

Next, Tezcatlipoca turns up in Tollan disguised as a warrior and invites the people to come to the gardens there. When they turn up, he attacks them with a hoe. Most of those that he fails to kill crush each other to death in the panic to escape.

Another of Tezcatlipoca's ruses was to appear in the market place showing off a miniature child whom he holds in the palm of his hand. The child (who is really the war god Huitzilopochtli) obeys his instructions to dance and leap about on Tezcatlipoca's hand. A crowd of Toltecs gathers to watch and, as their numbers swell, and they push forward eagerly to get a better view, many of them are killed in the crush.

The Toltecs are angry and Tezcatlipoca goads them into stoning him and Huitzilipochtli to death, but the gods' bodies give out such noxious fumes that thousands of the Toltecs are infected and die of the plague. They decide they had better remove the gods before they do more damage, and they wind ropes round the bodies of the gods. The ropes suddenly break, and the people pulling them collapse on top of each other and are suffocated.

The myth of Huitzilopochtli

This god was the Aztec's own tribal sun god, and the god of war. He is depicted with his limbs painted blue, hummingbird feathers tied around his leg and his arrows tipped with downy feathers. He is associated with hummingbirds because they were thought to be the souls of warriors who had been killed in battle; they accompany their sun god as he crosses the sky each day.

The water goddess Coatlicue is on the mountain of Coatapec (near Tollan) when a ball of brightly coloured, downy feathers falls from the sky and lands on her breast, magically impregnating her. When her daughter Coyolxauhqui and her 400 sons hear that their mother is pregnant, they think she has disgraced them utterly and they plot to kill her.

Coatlicue is frightened, but the spirit of her unborn child visits her and tells her not to worry. Coyolxauhqui leads her brothers on a march to find and kill their mother who is on the mountain. As they reach the beleaguered Coatlicue, her son Huitzilopochtli springs from the womb fully formed (like the Greek goddess Athena), and painted blue, and beheads his sister Coyolxauhqui. He throws her body down the mountian, and then kills his 400 brothers.

In some versions Huitzilopochtli throws his sister's head up into the sky where it becomes the moon (he himself being the sun), and his 400 brothers become the stars.

6

THE MODERN MYTH

It seems that the need for myths and stories is universal to the human race. We still want heroes whom we tell exaggerated stories about to glorify their courage or cleverness, and we still want to hear stories about characters whom we know, who set us examples of good or bad behaviour. Even those people who do not belong to a religion or believe in a god still co-operate by listening to and perpetuating these modern myths.

A good example of a modern myth is the story of Sir Francis Drake winning the battle of the Spanish Armada off the south coast of England in 1588. According to the popular story, the English had a tiny fleet but managed to beat the mighty Armada against all the odds through courage and ingenuity. The facts, on the other hand, are that the English had 197 ships to Spain's 130, and the Armada was completely becalmed, unable to do anything. The only grain of truth in the story is that although the English fleet was larger than the Spanish fleet, the ships themselves were a lot smaller. That's why they were so much more manoeuvrable and effective.

Another even more recent example is the myth that the British beat the Luftwaffe in the Battle of Britain in 1940 because the British planes were so much better designed and their pilots were more skilled and more courageous. This is a great example of a hero myth that helps to bind a nation together and inspire other fighters to show the same bravery and determination.

Once again, the truth is rather different. There is no doubt that the British pilots were extremely highly trained and showed huge courage. But the same is true of the Nazis. The fact is that the British nearly lost the air battle. The only thing that saved them was that the Germans made a huge tactical error and changed their strategy. They stopped bombing the air bases in south-east England and started to bomb civilian targets instead. Tragic as the results were for the British, it nevertheless saved them the war.

As for the modern equivalent of gods and goddesses, the pantheons of the late twentieth century are provided by the television soap operas. They give us a constant cast of regular characters whom we know well, and whose stories and relationships we follow. They bind us together – we can share them and discuss them with complete strangers – and their behaviour functions as a kind of moral tuning-fork. We can all agree that 'He shouldn't have done that' or 'She deserves some luck; she's been through so much'.

So our need for myth continues, even in the technological age, when scientists are giving us accounts of the creation that are intended to remove all the mystery (and which, in many cases, are remarkably similar to the mythical explanations of many ancient civilisations). And 4,500 years after the Mesopotamians first wrote down the epic of Gilgamesh, we still recognise it as a damn good story with an enduring message to tell us.

INDEX